GETTIN' OLD
AIN'T FOR WIMPS

KAREN O'CONNOR

HARVEST HOUSE PUBLISHERS
EUGENE, OREGON

Scripture quotations are taken from the HOLY BIBLE, NEW INTERNATIONAL VERSION®. NIV®. Copyright © 1973, 1978, 1984 Biblica, Inc.™ Used by permission of Zondervan. All rights reserved.

Cover by Dugan Design Group

Published in association with the literary agency of Janet Kobobel Grant, Books & Such, 4788 Carissa Avenue, Santa Rosa, California 95405

Every effort has been made to give proper credit for all stories, poems, and quotations. If for any reason proper credit has not been given, please notify the author or publisher and proper notation will be given on future printings.

GETTIN' OLD AIN'T FOR WIMPS
Copyright © 2004 by Karen O'Connor
Published by Harvest House Publishers
Eugene, Oregon 97408
www.harvesthousepublishers.com

Library of Congress Cataloging-in-Publication Data

O'Connor, Karen, 1938–
  Gettin' old ain't for wimps / Karen O' Connor.
    p. cm.
  ISBN 978-0-7369-7393-9 (Choice Exclusive)
  ISBN 978-0-7369-1476-5 (pbk.)
  ISBN 978-0-7369-3145-8 (eBook)
  1. Christian aged—Religious life. 2. Aging—Religious aspects—Christianity.
I. Title.
  BV4580.O355 2004
  248.8'5—dc22   2004003883

Printed in the United States of America.

20 21 22 / BP-KB / 11

For all the women in my life.
May we age with hope, humility, and humor.

.

Even to your old age and gray hairs I am he,
I am he who will sustain you.
I have made you and I will carry you;
I will sustain you and I will rescue you.

—Isaiah 46:4

Acknowledgments

The author wishes to thank the following men and women for sharing their funny experiences—many of which have been woven into the fabric of this book—and for permission to use their names where appropriate.

Donna Adee • Barbara Anson • Millie Barger • Bea Beeman • Kathy Boyle • Nancy Parker Brummett • Sue Buchanan • Barbara Jean Camp • Janice Chaffee • Dolores Collins • Candy Davison • Mona Downey • Marilou Flinkman • Charles Flowers • Susan M. Foster • Susan Fox • Freda Fullerton • Debbie Garner • Paul Gauntt • Millie Gess • Ginny Gielow • Cheryl Griffith • Janet Hawkins • Donna Hill • Nancy Ellen Hird • Roger Howell • Kathy Humber • Shelley Hussey • Jerilyn Jackson • Diana L. James • Sherry Lee James • B.J. Jensen • Mary Jenson • Alice J. Joy • Olga Kenney • Judy Kimball • Jean Klein • Margaret Krauss • Angela Kuenzler • Jim Lamb • Carmen Leal • Carole Lewis • Joan Lucas • Deanna Luke • Teri Marriott • Nona Michaud • Lynn D. Morrissey • Sharon L. Patterson • Cindy Plewinski • Betty Chapman Plude • Marilyn R. Prasow • Mary Beth Robb • Karen Robertson • Peggy Matthews-Rose • Carol Russell • Starla Ryan • Joyce Seaboldt • Wendy Shumaker • Margaret Speer • Maureen Stirsman • Susan Stonitsch • Karen Stringfield • Jack Swanson • Lettie Sweazy • Diana Wallis Taylor • Pam Trask • Cindy Vander Haar • June Varnum • Jeanne Warnke • Lonnie West • Debbie Wong • Connie Bertelsen Young • Jeanne Zornes

Contents

Yes, I'm a Senior Citizen!

I'm the life of the party—even if it lasts until 8 P.M.

I'm very good at opening childproof caps—with a hammer.

I'm usually interested in going home before I get to where I am going.

I'm awake many hours before my body allows me to get up.

I'm smiling all the time because I can't hear a thing you're saying.

I'm very good at telling stories over and over and over and over...

I'm aware that other people's grandchildren are not nearly as cute as mine.

I'm so cared for—long term care, eye care, private care, dental care.

—AUTHOR UNKNOWN

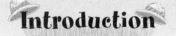

Introduction

My husband and I were browsing in a gift shop during a visit to Lexington, Kentucky. A plaque on the wall caught my eye:

DON'T COMPLAIN ABOUT GROWING OLD...

FEW PEOPLE GET THE PRIVILEGE!

We smiled at the wisdom of those few words. How blessed we felt in that moment—to realize we had successfully reached our sixth and seventh decades and were still kicking and laughing. I suddenly got excited about all the possibilities still ahead—adventures, risks, funny experiences, the "stuff" of life that keeps us young at heart regardless of the circumstances.

That "stuff" is the heart of this book. I hope you'll enjoy the humorous stories and inspirations included here, each one tied to a real-life incident—as well as the scriptures and prayers so that by the time you finish reading, you'll agree that getting old ain't for wimps! It's for people like you and me, who want to keep on loving, living, and laughing all the way home to the Father's house—the one He has prepared for us.

Karen O'Connor
San Diego, California

Risky
Business

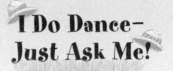

I Do Dance— Just Ask Me!

My friend Lynn, who recently toppled into her fifties, admits that she now does some things spontaneously that she might not have done years ago. One of them is dancing to praise music in the privacy of her own home.

One day while whirling and dipping through the living room as the music wafted from the stereo, she suddenly noticed that her daughter Sheridan's young friend Austin was watching wide-eyed and wide-mouthed.

"What are you doing?" he asked.

"Why, dancing, of course," she replied. "Would you and Sheridan like to join me? She often does."

"My mother doesn't dance," Austin said soberly. "And you're too old to dance!"

"I've never been much of a dancer," Lynn admitted, when relating this incident to me. "But I'll keep trying—even without the encouragement of Austin and others—including my husband, Mike. His response—an echo of Fred Astaire's comment to Ginger Rogers—never varies: 'I don't dance; don't ask me.'"

Lynn recalled that at wedding receptions, "after stilted attempts at slow dancing (though he was skilled at stepping on my feet), Mike would literally shove me into other couples,

13

admonishing loudly enough for everyone to hear: 'Lynni, stop pushing!' "

These occurrences escalated until, as Lynn put it, "they reached one final, humiliating climax." Lynn's boss was retiring and invited her and Michael to a special celebration—at a disco-restaurant, no less!

"After dinner, couples gathered under bright lights and a spinning, mirrored globe. Upon my repeated urgings," said Lynn, "Michael reluctantly followed me, but before stepping onto the floor he whispered this warning into my ear: 'Lynni, this sounds like one of those songs that starts out slow and ends up fast, and if it does, I am sitting down.'"

After hearing a few notes, Michael seemed to know what was coming. The song was slow at first, then the pace picked up. As promised (or threatened, maybe?), Michael left the dance floor and sat down.

But Lynn did not. "I stood speechless, motionless, incredulous—mortified!" she said. She couldn't believe her husband would stoop so low as to leave her to solo! "I tried to escape," she said, "but I was bumped from one rump to the next!"

Lynn groped her way through the gyrating group, suddenly realizing that most of the dancers were no more skilled than she was. Many danced without a partner and seemed to be having a better time on their own.

Lynn took their cue, kicked up her heels, and danced the night away. "Since that evening long ago, I have learned to dance," said Lynn with a smile. "Just ask me." And she feels perfectly at ease doing so. Why even King David danced in praise of the Lord!

As for Michael? Well he has not been able to sit on the sidelines for long. Now that his daughter Sheridan is becoming a young lady, she invites him each year to Cupid's Ball at the Ritz–Carlton Hotel. How could he refuse his own child? "He still doesn't dance (Oh, please don't ask him!)," said Lynn, "but Sheridan doesn't seem to know the difference!"

Reflection

Let them praise his name with dancing and make music to him with tambourine and harp (Psalm 149:3).

Talking to God

Dear Lord, sometimes I feel a little clumsy on my feet, especially as I get older. But you don't judge me by my ability to kick up my heels! You smile when I dance in your presence—even if in spirit only.

Is It Contagious?

Jeanne Z., age 56, is wondering if forgetfulness is a contagious disease. Can she catch it from her 83-year-old mother-in-law who lives next door? If proximity to the transmitter is any indication, then Jeanne better watch out! Almost daily she is involved with Mrs. Zornes on her safari for lost keys, misplaced bills, or V.I.T.s—Very Important Things.

One evening when her husband came home from work, Jeanne relayed to him the latest "lost" escapade that had occurred next door. He listened patiently—but clearly he had something else on his mind. He admitted it. He was hungry for pumpkin pie and more interested in having Jeanne satisfy that urge than hearing about another episode of his mother's forgetfulness.

There was nothing they could do about Mom! Jeanne would take her mind off that situation by focusing on making the pie. She opened the pantry and discovered she had just what she needed—a can of pumpkin puree and a can of evaporated milk.

"Give me an hour, honey," she said, "and I'll have it ready." Jeanne hurried to the kitchen, threw the ingredients into a bowl, rolled out a crust, and popped it into the oven, proud that she had made all this happen within the time frame promised—and after a stressful day at that.

Her husband sat down to a slice of warm pie and picked up his fork with a smile of satisfaction. He took a bite…then suddenly grimaced.

"Did you forget something?" he asked. "It's not sweet like it usually is."

Jeanne took a bite and had to admit he was correct. She checked the recipe: Oops! 3/4 cup of sugar.

She handed him the sugar bowl. "Here," she said, "just sprinkle on some sugar and pretend."

Jeanne was sure, then, that she had been hanging out with her mother-in-law too much. Maybe she did pick up the "forgetfulness" bug after all!

Reflection

Cast your cares on the LORD and he will sustain you (Psalm 55:22).

Talking to God

Dear Lord, little episodes of forgetfulness are amusing—especially when I take them with a grain of sugar! But sometimes they scare me. I wonder if I'm losing touch. At such times, remind me to turn to you right away. You will hold me close because, like no other, you care for me just as I am.

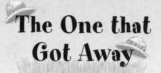

The One that Got Away

Marilou and her husband, son, and her son's friend settled into a rented cabin in the backwoods of Alaska. Their water supply came from a stream nearby and the bathroom—well, it was an outhouse up a winding path.

The men had brought in their supplies by boat and were ready to do some serious fishing. They had come to catch salmon—as had the bears!

"The bears fished on one side of the stream, and we fished the other," said Marilou.

"That night," she added, "I woke up with my usual need to go to the bathroom. As quietly as possible, I crept outside and up the path to the outhouse. On my way back, I missed the last step on the porch and fell against a bench holding a lantern. The lantern shattered."

Within seconds three men burst out of the cabin door.

"Fortunately for me," said Marilou, "they looked first—*before* shooting the bear they expected to see on the porch. Instead, their flashlights illuminated a little old lady—me—in flannel pajamas and boots."

After much teasing, Marilou crawled back into her bunk. The next evening as she went to bed, there on her pillow, lined up in a row, were three flashlights!

Reflection

Though he stumble, he will not fall, for the
LORD upholds him with his hand (Psalm 37:24).

Talking to God

*O God of my salvation, if it weren't for you I
don't know what I would do! I'd fall a thousand
times a day—and not just over a step or a curb,
but into fear, anxiety, or worry. When I read your
promise, though, I realize I'd never fall into such
traps again if I hung onto your strong hand and
never let go. Lord, I want to walk hand-in-hand
with you for the rest of my days.*

Leaping Lizard!

Debbie's mother rented a home in Fallbrook, California. Unfortunately, the house had several "leaks" around the doorways and windows, as many older stucco houses do. One day while she was home alone and busy with her daily routine, she noticed something dark on the carpet. She leaned over for a closer look and to her surprise, it was a lizard lying motionless.

"My mother is very afraid of frogs, snakes, and lizards," said Debbie, "yet she didn't want to kill the little creature. She ran into the kitchen, grabbed a large cooking pot, and returned to the scene. She popped the pot over the lizard like a lid until her husband could return from work and take care of it.

She kept a close watch, worried, however, that if the lizard did slip out he might bite her. One couldn't be too cautious, you know! Just in case, she climbed up on a chair and never moved until her husband walked through the door.

"My dad was rather surprised to see Mom perched on a chair," Debbie commented as she laughed, "staring at the pot on the floor in front of her."

Moments later, he had heard the full story and started laughing. "You know that lizard you thought you captured

20

under the pot?" he asked with a twinkle in his eye. "Well, it's sitting under your chair."

Apparently the lizard decided to protect itself, too!

Reflection

My God is my rock, in whom I take refuge (Psalm 18:2).

Talking to God

O Lord, thank you for being the one solid, immovable rock in my life. When I run to you, I am safe, secure, and at peace. There is none like you.

Snakes Alive!

At age sixty-something, June moved from her home in the city to a rural area in Northern California.

"My husband of 41 years had passed away 8 years before, and I needed to rebuild my life," said June. "I'd never lived in the country, but a rural setting had always appealed to me and to my husband. Our favorite getaway was camping in the mountains by a stream or lake in a quiet meadow with tall pine trees and inviting places to explore."

June found a small house on a nice-sized plot of land with a gurgling creek running alongside the backyard. "My city-dwelling garden tools," said June, "gave way to a backhoe and tractor."

However, her shovel could not begin to budge the buried rocks and large boulders that she discovered when she started planting trees. A kind neighbor brought in his tractor. "A six-foot wire fence soon replaced the low fence," said June, "as I tried to keep the deer from eating my new trees, shrubs, and flowers."

But deer were not the only visitors. Three raccoons and a skunk stopped by nearly every day. "I watched them tip-toeing across my backyard," said June. "I had to laugh as I watched them sneak along, probably hoping I wouldn't notice."

She also learned to put the trash barrel in the garage, so the resident bears didn't investigate the contents. "I'd never met a bear in person," said June, "and I sure didn't want to now."

One afternoon, June discovered a huge snake curled around the railing of her back porch. "I tried not to scream or faint," June said with a smile, "as I slid back into the house. Who could I call for help? No one was around. I prayed, then gathered my courage, and slipped out the door, hugging the wall so the snake wouldn't see me. I walked into the garage and grabbed the rake. I was shaking so hard, I almost dropped it. But I snagged the snake and prayed it wouldn't climb up the handle while I raced out the back gate and over to the creek."

Thankfully, the snake dislodged itself from the tines of the rake and slithered into the weeds.

"And don't you ever come back!" she shouted after it. "The rake stayed by the back door for a few days—just in case," said June.

Reflection

Do not be terrified; do not be discouraged, for the LORD your God will be with you wherever you go (Joshua 1:9).

Talking to God

Lord, what a great promise! You encourage me to go, to do, to participate in life regardless of my age. And you don't limit my creativity or curiosity. In fact, you put only two restrictions on me—don't be terrified and don't be discouraged. Great! Right now I'm leaving this baggage behind. I don't need anything but the assurance that wherever I go you'll be right there with me.

Missing Dentures

Diana and her husband moved from Southern California to Northern California. They also settled Diana's 83-year-old mother into a small house nearby. A girlfriend, Nonie, from their previous community, came to visit Diana so the two women stopped by to say hello to Diana's mother.

"We found her in a very agitated state," said Diana. "Both her upper and lower dentures were missing, and she didn't know what happened to them."

They suspected Pierre, the little dog. He liked to take things off Diana's mother's night table. "Nonie and I began a frantic search of the house," said Diana. "We looked in every spot where Pierre might have hidden them. Finally, in the yard I found fresh dirt, and sure enough I uncovered the upper plate. The dog hadn't chewed it up, so after a thorough scrubbing with some disinfectant, Mother fitted it into her mouth."

The lower dentures, however, were still missing. After two hours of searching the house and yard for the second time, Diana and Nonie gave up.

"I told Mother I'd make a dental appointment to have a new one made. We said good-bye and returned home," said Diana. "Nonie and I had no sooner gotten in the front door when the phone rang. It was my mother. She giggled nervously and finally confessed she had found her lower plate.

"It is so comfortable," her mother said with an embarrassed laugh, "that I forgot it was in my mouth!"

Reflection

Do not fear disgrace; you will not be humiliated (Isaiah 54:4).

Talking to God

These embarrassing moments seem to be adding up lately. I'm forgetting this, losing track of that. It would be so easy to give up, keep quiet, drop out of sight. But I refuse to do that! You told me clearly not to be afraid of disgrace. I'm going to take you at your word, Lord! Some may look at me with judgment as I grow older, but you don't. In your eyes I'm never someone to be ashamed of.

Ahem...
Your Zipper!

I've never been able to carry a tune," said Pastor Jim. "I guess I'm what people call tone deaf. The sad thing is I really do love to sing. But now that I'm over 60, my ability to croon a tune has become even worse."

One Sunday, Jim related, the person who usually gave the announcements and called the congregation to worship was nowhere around. Jim couldn't find a substitute on such short notice, so he decided to fill the gap himself.

"This meant standing behind the pulpit," he said, "following the usual sequence of events, and then singing as the worship leader led us in song."

During the second song of the series, suddenly the woman leading worship stopped singing. She turned to Pastor Jim, and in front of everyone, stated firmly, "You have got to stop singing. You are completely throwing me off."

The congregation turned stone silent. Jim didn't know what to do. So he dropped his head, pretending to be deeply wounded, and stepped down from the platform. The congregation erupted into laughter! Jim assumed they enjoyed his playful response to the rude remark.

"I walked back a few aisles and found an empty seat in a pew," said Jim. "I extended my hand to a woman there and

26

asked if I could stand next to her and sing the rest of the songs."

They sang, sat down for a moment, then stood to sing again. "Then I realized," said Jim, "that it was drafty in the area in front of my brand-new pants."

He looked down and saw that his zipper had probably popped open when he stepped off the platform. So *that* was the cause of all the laughter. Jim turned on a dime toward the windows and pulled the zipper up quickly to close it.

And what became of the pastor's pants? "I never wore them again," he said with a good laugh.

Reflection

Fear of man will prove to be a snare, but whoever trusts in the LORD is kept safe (Proverbs 29:25).

Talking to God

When I start focusing on what other people think of me instead of what you think of me, O Lord, I'm in trouble! Right then I need to slow down, take a deep breath, and remember your promise. Fear of man will take me down; trust in you will keep me safe.

Sticky Situation

Kathy received a lighthouse wind chime for Christmas one year from her sister. "When I opened the box several days later, I noticed the lighthouse had become separated from the strings and chimes."

Kathy and her mother spent two hours trying to pull the tangled strings apart. "I was sure I had the solution," said Kathy. "I bought some Super Glue so I could attach the base to the chimes. I glued the top part of the circular piece of wood that held the strings, then put the lighthouse on top of that."

So far so good. Kathy said she discovered that if she turned the lighthouse upside down the glue would keep the strings together. She stood still for a few moments holding the lighthouse right side up with the chimes hanging down.

Not a good idea.

"My finger stuck to the glue on the side of the base. No wonder it is called Super Glue," said Kathy. "I tugged on my finger but it wouldn't budge. And it hurt! I got a sharp knife and slowly pried my finger away from the glue and wind chime. I only lost a little skin from the top layer, thank goodness. Now I know to pay attention—at all times—to what I'm doing!"

Reflection

In all your ways acknowledge him, and he will make your paths straight (Proverbs 3:6).

Talking to God

Lord, how easy it is to stay on the straight and narrow. All it takes is keeping you foremost in my mind at all times and in all ways. You'd think I'd want to make a habit of it! But how quickly I forget. I have gotten myself into some pretty sticky situations. Thank you for being patient with me and for loving me even when I am foolish or weak.

Supergram!

In 1977, the year before the birth of the triathlon in Hawaii, Margaret S. says she was "fat, 40, and a couch potato," with a husband who decided *they* needed to get in shape by participating in a triathlon—an athletic event that includes swimming, bicycling, and running.

"The Hawaii race," explained Margaret, "is a 2.4-mile open-water ocean swim, a 112-mile bicycle ride up to Havee and back, topped off with a 26.2-mile marathon run with a cut-off time of 17 hours."

Margaret, however, encountered a big problem before they even started. "I was afraid of water," she said. But that didn't stop her. Margaret received help from a water safety instructor, a promise from God that she need not have a spirit of fear, and encouragement from her husband, Jack, that she could do whatever she set her mind on. Feeling fortified on all fronts, Margaret committed to becoming fit.

"For my first triathlon race," she said, "I borrowed a cut-off wet suit with just enough flotation in it to convince me I wouldn't drown. The one-mile swim took me longer than anyone else. Why? I did all of it on my back—swimming a lot further than others because I couldn't see where I was going!"

When Margaret finally came out of the water, one of her running friends who served as a volunteer told her she had been out there so long doing the dead man's float that people started thinking she really was dead.

At another event, Margaret encountered yet another challenge. The female swimmers competed first. Before they were finished, however, the gun went off for the men to start. Most of them were strong and aggressive swimmers, and they could easily overtake most of the women—especially Margaret.

By that time in her fitness program, Margaret could put her face in the water and swim a few strokes before gasping for air. But, she admitted, she still struggled to keep afloat and move forward at the same time.

"Suddenly," she said, "someone behind me was splashing hard. Then a hand hit the back of my leg as a big, hairy, male body swam right over the top of me. I shoved him as hard as I could and screamed, 'GET OFF ME!' "

A lot of good that did! "That rude animal just kept swimming *and* kicked me as he swam by. I was really angry, but I didn't let that stop me from finishing the race and winning the trophy for my age group."

Later that day as Margaret and Jack drove back to their home, they compared stories about their race experiences. "I told Jack about the big, hairy guy who swam right over the top of me." His look spoke a thousand words. "Oh, was that you?" he blurted out—perhaps sorry he had let on.

"Our marriage survived that episode and more," said Margaret. "In 1988, we crossed the finish line at the Hawaii World Championship Triathlon in just 16 hours. I am forever indebted to my husband for helping me change from a fat, 40-year-old couch potato to an energetic, enthusiastic, smiling triathlete."

Reflection

Let us run with perseverance the race marked out for us (Hebrews 12:1).

Talking to God

It's so encouraging, Lord, to read about people who have made such dramatic changes in their lives. It can be a bit intimidating! But only if I dwell on their accomplishments and forget that you have a "race" marked for me, too. It may not be a track-and-field event, but it will be just right for this time in my life. Lead the way, Lord, and I'll follow.

Auto Mania

Icebreaker

At one time in Carmen's professional life she worked for a man she dubbed Mr. You-Produce-and-I'll-Take-All-the-Credit.

"But to give him his due," said Carmen, "he did one thing well. He knew how to delegate quickly and easily. He told me to do everything, and he would do nothing."

One morning while Carmen was filling in for him—once again—she was required "to give a major presentation to a group of high-level, crème de la crème potential customers."

It was an important program designed to whet their appetites for the cell phones the company was selling—at a time when such a product was brand-new to the market. This was not Carmen's "show," and she resented having to take her boss' place. The event was scheduled at a hotel adjacent to the largest mall in Hawaii during the week before Christmas. "Parking was at a premium," said Carmen, "and traffic was what you'd expect during a holiday season."

At the time, the company was in its infancy, and there were fewer than 12 cell phones completed and working. "One perk to being a manager," said Carmen, "was that I had a phone and used it often. But service was not going to be open to the public until June. Back then I used a car phone rather than a portable."

That particular day, Carmen pulled into a parking slot, and then continued talking on the car phone, which required that she keep the keys in the ignition. After completing her conversation, she hung up, slid out of the driver's seat, and slammed the door. *Oh no!* She suddenly realized she had locked herself out. And there on the passenger seat were "my literature, business cards, and everything else I needed for my speech," said Carmen, "within sight but out of reach. I panicked."

But then she remembered the hatchback was unlocked. "Great," she mumbled. "All I have to do is crawl over the seat, grab the keys, and hurry into the hotel to get this program over with." However, crawling into a hatchback space in full business attire, including pantyhose, proved to be a challenge, especially when she remembered that she had not worn underwear over her stockings in order to prevent the outline of the panties showing through her dress!

"As I shimmied into the car and over the seats," said Carmen, "my dress rode up around my waist. Though I honestly tried to pull it down as I went, I couldn't use too much force because I was afraid of ripping it."

Then suddenly a booming voice caught her attention. "I don't know whether to arrest you for breaking-and-entering or for indecent exposure," a young police officer barked, trying to contain his laughter. Then he asked Carmen to step out of the car—that is, if she *could!*

"You see, officer," Carmen began, after managing to extricate herself and pulling her dress back to where it belonged, "I was in my car, talking on the phone when…"

The expression on his face told Carmen immediately that he didn't believe a word she was saying. Cell phones were simply not part of the norm as they are today. It took some time to persuade the officer to unlock the doors and let Carmen prove her case.

As she waited for his verdict, a gathering crowd looked on and seemed to be enjoying this embarrassing moment. "Once I'd convinced him that I wasn't some sort of exhibitionist," added Carmen, "I retrieved the car phone and showed it to the policeman as well as to the crowd."

Carmen decided to join in the fun that everyone else appeared to be having, so she made a few jokes of her own and then passed out business cards galore!

The police officer did not write her a ticket, and everyone had a great laugh at Carmen's expense—everyone except her, that is. "If I can just get through this day," she muttered, "I'm going to quit. But first I'm going to tell off Mr. You-Know-Who!"

But Carmen never got the opportunity! When she walked into the hotel meeting room, she received a standing ovation—even before she opened her mouth! "Apparently a large number of men from the audience had caught my act in the parking lot!" said Carmen. "Talk about an ice-breaker!"

Carmen said it turned out to be one of the best sales presentations she'd ever made, and ultimately she sold many phones "to people who first viewed the phone while viewing me!"

Reflection

I will turn the darkness into light before them and make the rough places smooth (Isaiah 42:16).

Talking to God

Lord, you, better than anyone, know how dark some of my hours have been. I've had my share of frustrations at home, at work, and right here on my own street. People seem to get a kick out of watching others get into predicaments that make them look stupid or helpless. Good for a quick laugh, maybe, but ultimately pretty cruel. I am so thankful you are here to turn on the light and smooth out the rough spots.

Parking Lot Panic

Nona had made several trips to JCPenney's in the local mall not far from where she lives. She was excited about placing an order for new drapes for a bedroom in her home.

One day she received a call from a customer service rep telling her the order was in. She rushed over to pick up the drapes, then hurried home to open the package. Oh no! They were the wrong color.

"I jumped into the car and drove back—disappointed and disgusted," she said. "In my frustration, I parked at the door on the west side of the store, forgetting that I usually park at the south entrance near the Customer Service Department."

Nona returned the drapes and placed a new order for the correct color. Then she hurried out the south entrance. There were only a few cars parked there, and nowhere did she see her brand-new Lincoln Town Car.

"I stood still for a moment, talking to myself in disbelief and near panic. I spotted a policeman near the west side parking lot and ran over to him for help. I was ready to report a stolen car—mine! About two cars to the left of him, there sat my car, right where I had parked it!"

Nona pulled herself together and tossed up a spontaneous prayer: "Thank you, Lord, for parking that policeman at the right place at the right time, and for keeping me from engaging in what was sure to be a very embarrassing moment."

Reflection

Whether you turn to the right or to the left, your ears will hear a voice behind you, saying, "This is the way; walk in it" (Isaiah 30:21).

Talking to God

Lord, what a sight it must be as we scurry around, confused about this and worried about that. I know that my life would be a lot easier if I stopped and listened to you before I run off trying to solve things on my own. Thank you for not giving up on me, and for reminding me, when I do listen, when to turn right and when to turn left.

Stolen Car

Garnet drove to a small shopping center near home to mail some packages. When she came out of the store, she couldn't find her car anywhere. She looked up and down the rows, but none of the vehicles were hers. Her heart pounded.

Her daughter Linda suddenly drove into the lot, and Garnet rushed up to her, relieved and panicked at the same time.

"Mom! What are you doing?" Linda asked, worried. Her mother looked a bit dazed. *Had she fallen—or worse, been hit by a car?* Linda wondered.

"My car's been stolen!" Garnet shouted. "It was right here," she said, pointing to the spot where she was certain she had left it. "And now it's gone!" She climbed into Linda's car in tears.

"Maybe you forgot where you parked it?" Linda asked in a sympathetic tone. "Let's look together." She drove up and down the rows slowly so as not to overlook even one automobile. Garnet insisted that she knew where her car had been parked. Linda wasn't so sure that her mother was remembering correctly.

Finally, Linda gave in. She agreed with her mother. The only recourse was to phone the police and report the stolen car. Just then Garnet's husband came tooling into the parking lot—driving *her* car!

He pulled up beside his wife and daughter with a sheepish grin on his face. "I came down to pick up some groceries and must have forgotten which car I took. When I came out, I saw this car, got in, and drove home. When I pulled up in front of our house, I suddenly realized I drove home in a different car than I had left in."

Then he parked Garnet's auto, walked two rows over to *his* car, got in, and drove off.

I'm curious about what went on behind closed doors when Garnet finally made it home in her own vehicle!

Reflection

He guides the humble in what is right and teaches them his way (Psalm 25:9).

Talking to God

Other people can make us hopping mad sometimes—especially those we love the most! I'm wondering if you could say the same thing about me, dear God. But you're not given to fits of anger over simple mistakes. You guide me...when I'm humble enough to cut my family and friends a little slack. Then you show me what is right, and you teach me your ways. I'm so grateful for you, O Lord.

Driving Mom Nuts

At 82, Inez is doing pretty well. She takes Coumadin for a heart rhythm problem, but she can still get around and even drive. At 88, her husband, S.J., has not driven in five years—at least behind the wheel. He drives from the passenger seat—directing Inez all over town!

One day he said he wanted to go to the store for a loaf of bread. He had a certain sandwich in mind, and he needed the right bread. Inez was tired and wanted him to wait till the next day. "Let's pick up a loaf tomorrow when we go to the bank and post office," she said.

"I want to go now!" S.J. demanded.

Inez waved him off, certain he would come to his senses and realize there was no rush on this one small errand.

S.J. went out the back door.

A few moments later, Inez looked around for her husband. It wasn't like him to be too far from sight. As she glanced out the window she noticed that her bright-red Cadillac was missing. She hurried to the front door and opened it just in time to see S.J. driving down their street.

Inez panicked. She called her sister to report what had happened. "S.J. just drove off to go to the grocery store!" she cried, stunned.

Her sister suggested she and her sister's son who was visiting, follow right behind him.

Next, Inez called her daughter Karen. "Your father has driven off in my car!" Karen, who lived about 20 minutes away, told her mother to stay put and pray! She'd be right over. Karen could tell her mother was worried and anxious.

Inez and her nephew returned without S.J. They caught up with him at the store but he seemed to be doing just fine so they left him there. About 10 minutes later, S.J. pulled into the driveway. He had purchased the bread he wanted as well as a few other items. He proceeded to make the sandwich he had been hankering for.

And Inez? Well, by that time she needed a blood-pressure pill!

Reflection

But here is the bread that comes down from heaven, which a man may eat and not die (John 6:50).

Talking to God

Funny how when we make up our minds to do something we're gung ho till we get it done! Hmmm! Maybe that's the problem. We look for our daily bread in all the wrong places. But you provide the bread that leads to eternal life in heaven.

Perfect Crime

One weekend evening, a tall, clean-cut young man knocked on Mona and Jim Downey's patio door in The Residency, where they lived in Scottsbluff, Nebraska.

"Have you seen a short, red-headed, older lady who works as a hair dresser in a salon on Broadway?" he asked.

The man didn't know her name, and he seemed evasive when the Downeys spoke to him. They urged him to check with a staff person in the office when it opened the following Monday morning.

The couple then left their apartment for an outing at the Scottsbluff Country Club. They walked to the parking garage where their Suburban vehicle and Mona's "new" used white Lincoln were parked. They decided to take the Lincoln, which was a gift from Jim to Mona for her sixty-seventh birthday.

First stop, the Platte Valley National Bank ATM to withdraw some cash. When Jim returned to the car he noticed the trunk and gas cap release buttons on the floor by the driver's seat. *How odd,* he thought. He had never noticed them before. He assumed these were features peculiar to the '89 Lincoln.

Jim asked Mona to turn up the volume on the radio. It was so low, he couldn't hear it. "I don't think we had it on,"

Mona commented. Then as she reached in the dark for the familiar power switch and volume control she couldn't find either one.

They arrived at the country club and Jim dropped off Mona at the front door, but she had trouble finding the door latch. He then parked at the far end of the lot next to a white Suburban. The couple enjoyed a leisurely dinner with friends and watched a movie.

At the end of the evening Mona and Jim walked out to the parking lot, but couldn't locate their car anywhere. They spotted a white Suburban and two other newer model white cars but not theirs.

Finally, in desperation, Jim called 9-1-1 to report the missing car. "The operator asked for everything but my blood type," Jim said, feeling a bit worked over. A deputy arrived, and Jim filled him in on all the details—the missing car, the mysterious young man who knocked on their patio door, and a trio of loud mouths who after a fight, roared off in a white car on the highway near the entrance to the country club.

The deputy took control and contacted the local police, asking that an officer check the parking garage at The Residency. He discovered that another vehicle had been stolen from the same parking structure. It was a white '91 Mercury, which belonged to Mike Marsden, a young man visiting his parents who also lived at The Residency. At that moment the Downeys realized it was the same Mercury they were standing next to in the row where their own Lincoln had been!

A police officer called the deputy on the radio. The stolen Lincoln had been found—in the lot in front of The Residency. Two more squad cars arrived at the country club and as people were leaving the club for home, they passed by and offered the Downeys their condolences.

By 10:30 P.M., everyone was exhausted from the long drama. An officer drove Mona and Jim back to The Residency in his squad car. Immediately they checked the Lincoln—parked right next to the Suburban, as usual. Nothing missing. No exterior damage. The engine was cold. An officer then asked Mona an embarrassing question.

"Ma'am, are you sure you and your husband drove the Lincoln to the club?"

"Of course we did," she responded, feeling insulted.

The Mercury was returned to Mike Marsden, the owner. The Downeys' Lincoln was safe and sound. The couple thanked everyone for their help and returned to their apartment.

Just before retiring for the night, Jim decided to call The Residency manager, Charley Gulley, to alert him of the car-stealing ring operating in and around the facility. He also called his son, Mike, and brought him up-to-date on the evening's events.

As Mona was about to drop off to sleep, she turned to her husband with a concerned expression. "Do you think the officer was onto something when he asked me if we were certain we drove the Lincoln to the club? Do you think maybe we didn't?"

"Well, there's one way to find out," said Jim. "If there is no gas tank release and trunk release on the floor of our car, then we'll know for sure."

Jim went out to their Lincoln, and returned with a look of chagrin on his face. Mona's car did not have releases on the floor. Jim Downey was the thief he had been chasing! He had committed the perfect crime. In the dark that night, he and Mona had mistaken Mike Marsden's white Mercury for their white Lincoln. The amazing part is that the Downeys' key fit Mike's car!

Jim returned to their apartment and confessed his crime to Mona. They both went into hysterics. They debated whether or not to 'fess up or simply let this escapade be their little secret. They decided it was too funny to hide from others, even if it left them looking a bit stupid.

Jim had one more round of tasks to complete before dropping off to sleep that night. He called the sheriff to confess, the Residency manager to explain, and his son to ease his mind. And the following morning he called Mike Marsden to ask for forgiveness!

Moral of the story, according to Jim? You can't get into an old folks' home any too soon!

Reflection

If we confess our sins, he is faithful and just and will forgive us our sins and purify us from all unrighteousness (1 John 1:9).

Talking to God

Dear Lord, sometimes I find it hard to apologize, yet I always feel better when I do. Pride crowds out humility, especially after I've made a mistake that I'm embarrassed about. Please help me to see what is right and true and just and to say "I'm sorry" when it is the right thing to do.

Aches and Pains

Plumbing Problems

Susan's mother had been discharged from the hospital and needed a few items at the pharmacy. Susan agreed to pick them up.

"I went to the drugstore and had the prescriptions filled," said Susan, "then purchased several over-the-counter medications, which the doctor had specified. Unfortunately, Colace, a stool softener, was not in stock."

Susan drove to a second pharmacy and soon had the item in hand. "The middle-aged female checker eyed me as well as the Colace," said Susan.

"You know what?" the woman asked sweetly, "you ought to try prune juice. It works wonders!"

"Oh, no," Susan blurted aloud, totally embarrassed. "It's not for me. You see, my mother was just discharged from the hospital and..."

The checker would not be silenced so easily. "When I was growing up," she went on, "I had continual problems with irregularity, and I became addicted to laxatives. So I had to give them up—cold turkey. And you know what? It was two weeks before I was able to get relief."

By then, all Susan wanted to do was leave—and in a hurry. She pulled her money from her wallet and handed a bill to the checker. *Why is this complete stranger confiding such a personal story to me?* Susan wondered.

"I understand that fiber in the diet helps, too," Susan offered, hoping that would end the conversation, and she could slip out the door with the Colace in a discreet brown paper bag.

Sue returned home and shared this amusing incident with her mother. "Oh, I just remembered," her mom exclaimed. "The nurse suggested that I drink warm prune juice."

The following morning, Susan returned to the grocery store for a few more items. Nestled among the boxes of cereal, the dozen eggs, and the carton of milk was a trusty bottle of prune juice. "I hoped it would escape the checker's notice," joked Susan.

That afternoon, her father, who did not care for the regular flavored Milk of Magnesia which they had on hand, asked Susan to purchase the mint-flavored variety the following day.

Once again, Susan returned to the store to purchase more laxative. As she left, she exhaled a huge sigh of relief. She had gotten out of the store this time without so much as a nod from the checker.

Later that day, with a wry grin, she told her mother, "Gosh, Mom. Do you realize that I've had to purchase laxatives three days in a row? I sure hope I haven't earned an unwanted reputation in your town." They both laughed.

The following day Susan was bemused as she heard a pastor on the radio preach about *spiritual* constipation. "This condition occurs," he intoned, "when a Christian keeps taking in spiritual nourishment, but never gives out in service. After awhile, the individual becomes bloated and lethargic."

"I've got the perfect spiritual remedy," Susan quipped as she drove along. "Christian Colace, Miracle Milk of Magnesia, and Purifying Prune Juice!"

Reflection

Long life to you! Good health to you and your household! And good health to all that is yours! (1 Samuel 25:6).

Talking to God

Lord, I never thought about spiritual constipation before. But maybe I'm guilty of it. I realize that I often sit in church taking in all the nourishment provided—the worship music, the prayers for healing, your Word, the message of the week, and the friendship extended to me— yet, I am reluctant to step forward and offer my gifts. I want to change that thinking today. Please point me to the ministry where I can be most useful and content so I can give back some of what I have received.

Take These Bunions—Please!

I was trying my hardest to keep up, but I was no match for my grandmother when she was set on getting somewhere," said Jerilyn, recalling the many times she trekked along with her grandmother some 50 or more years ago. She walked as fast as her little legs could carry her, whether it was to the park, a rummage sale, a farmer's market on Thursdays, or to the amusement park at Long Beach Pike.

Occasionally, Jerilyn would spend the night with her grandmother. She remembers being fascinated with the woman's feet. To a little girl they seemed *ugly*.

"My grandmother had bunions," said Jerilyn, "something entirely new to me. From that time on I worried that my feet someday would look like hers.

"My grandmother has been gone for some time now, but I think about her often these days now that I have grandchildren of my own," Jerilyn continued. "Whenever I take them to lunch or to the park, I remember my time with Grandma at the Pike. I don't walk as much as she did; my grandkids and I usually go places by car. But even so, as I stare at my feet, I realize they look just like Grandma's. I now have bunions, too!"

Reflection

Since my youth, O God, you have taught me,
and to this day I declare your marvelous deeds
(Psalm 71:17).

Talking to God

*Lord, it's encouraging to read about other men
and women who are experiencing some of the
same challenges I am. I remember as a child
feeling invincible! But now I'm well aware of
how fragile life is and that mine could end at
any moment. That is why I want to continue
sharing all the marvelous things you have done
for me with others so they, too, can know the
wonder of your love.*

There Must Be a Pill for That

Candy was seated at her desk at work, with the phone handset propped between ear and shoulder as she listened to her husband describe a long-and-drawn-out conversation he had just had.

He is known for his "gift of gab," so Candy is used to listening to him. At one point in his monologue, she made a polite attempt to insert a comment. "But, Greg," she said, trying to make her point, "don't you remember that…"

"He carried right on," said Candy, "without even acknowledging me. How rude!"

Greg continued talking, and once again Candy attempted to get a word in edgewise. "But Greg," she insisted, "at Christmastime, don't you remember when Mom said…?"

Still he went on without so much as an extra breath. Candy suddenly worried. *He must be mad at me for some reason,* she thought. *He's doing this on purpose—not letting me say a word.*

Greg's words kept on flowing. After the third try Candy was about to give up. No point in going on when he persistently ignored her.

Then suddenly Candy woke up to what was happening. She was listening to his voice mail. "I forgot this was not a live conversation I was overhearing!"

Later, Candy reported this funny incident to Greg, who is seven years her junior and not yet a victim of senior moments! He smiled, looked at Candy, and said dryly, "Isn't there a pill you can take for that?"

Reflection

Do not gloat over me, my enemy! Though I have fallen, I will rise (Micah 7:8).

Talking to God

Lord, sometimes even my best friend or my spouse can seem like an enemy, especially if he or she pokes fun of me or teases me for something I've done that looks pretty foolish. But as I step back for a moment, maybe the best way to rise again is to join the laughter. I'm not perfect, and it's good to be reminded of it.

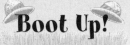

Boot Up!

Nancy cracked a bone in her right foot. The podiatrist put the foot into a padded boot with Velcro straps so she could take it off when necessary.

"The good news, and the bad news is that I don't have to wear it to bed," Nancy reported.

She can sleep comfortably without the confinement of the boot, but if she needs to get up in the middle of the night, she must put it back on.

"I suppose if I had the balance of a gymnast I could trek to the bathroom with a naked foot," joked Nancy. "On the other hand, if I had that kind of balance, I might not have cracked the bone in the first place!"

Nancy claims she is no gymnast; in fact, she says, "I'm a klutz!"

Each day she must carefully slide her injured foot into the boot, pull the tabs through the slots and snap them shut with the Velcro strap. Then she threads the straps that hold the tabs in place through their metal loops and secures them with Velcro.

At night, if she awakens to go to the bathroom, she must go through the same maneuvers. When she returns, she reverses the procedure before swinging her legs into bed.

The night after Halloween that same year, Nancy awakened at 2:30 and trekked to the bathroom, then got back in bed. Within seconds, she heard a mysterious creaking coming from the floor beside her bed. It sounded like Velcro! Who was there? Was someone hiding under the bed? Was she reacting to the ghost stories she had listened to the night before?

"Part of me wanted to turn on the flashlight and investigate," said Nancy. "But the scaredy-cat part won. I stayed put and shivered. I was about to wake up my husband, but decided to pray instead. I fell back to sleep, and the next thing I knew it was morning."

Later that day Nancy realized when she took the boot off and on, the straps could flop around when loosened vigorously, and if they fell too close to the Velcro they'd attach. That was the sound she had heard. What a relief!

Reflection

When you lie down, you will not be afraid; when you lie down, your sleep will be sweet (Proverbs 3:24).

Talking to God

How easily I am frightened, God, even by silly things like small noises in the night or shadows on the wall. My imagination goes wild right when I should be settling down for a deep rest. Thank you for the assurance that when I lie down I need not be afraid. You will give me a sweet sleep. Please remind me of this promise when I put my head on my pillow tonight.

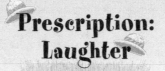

Prescription: Laughter

"There's something about a first appointment with a new doctor that's unnerving," admitted Nancy. "My long-time internist had announced his retirement, so I decided to take a chance on the new one. I scheduled a regular checkup."

As Nancy merged onto the interstate on her way to the medical suite, a cup of ice water in the cup holder of her car tipped over and splashed her.

"I attempted to soak up the water with a few tissues and drive at the same time. Not a good idea! The result was two wet seats—the car's and mine! I didn't want to be late so I drove on, praying that somehow my denim jumpsuit would dry out in the next few minutes."

Nancy signed in at the desk in the waiting room, holding her purse behind her so the other patients wouldn't notice her damp derriere. By the time the nurse called her into the examining room, Nancy couldn't keep quiet another moment. She confessed the episode, and the two had a good laugh.

The nurse tried to convince Nancy her wet pants were not that obvious, especially since denim is dark blue, but Nancy knew better the moment she stood up from the paper-covered examination table, which was now as wet as she was.

Nancy began imagining what would occur next. The new, younger doctor would come in, shake her hand, take one look and say, "Well, Mrs. Brummett, other than the incontinence, how are you handling growing older?"

The doctor, however, held his tongue. By the end of their initial visit, Nancy said she felt comfortable enough with him to confess her problem. She was encouraged to see that he could laugh about it, too!

Reflection

Our mouths were filled with laughter, our tongues with songs of joy (Psalm 126:2).

Talking to God

Lord, thank you for the gift of laughter. It is one of the best remedies for almost every crisis. I remember times when if I didn't laugh, I'd sit down and cry! Thank you for putting people in my life who know how to bring out the humor in almost anything. They show me the upside of a sad situation, and suddenly I see clearly again. I walk away smiling—even whistling sometimes.

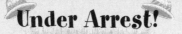

Under Arrest!

I openly confess," said Jack Swanson, "that I have been under arrest 14 times in the last two years—cardiac arrest, that is!"

Internal lightning struck during the Christmas holidays of 2001. Jack said he was perched on a chair in his wife's office pondering some writing he had done, when all of a sudden he was hit with a wave of nausea and dizziness. When he came to, he walked upstairs to report the incident to his family.

His eldest daughter, Krista, told her dad that when she had had a similar incident a doctor had diagnosed her as having vasovagal symptoms. "I didn't know a vasovagal from a bagel but at least she was still standing," said Jack, "and that made all the difference at the moment."

Jack's family suggested he call Dr. Jeff Gaver, a practicing physician, friend, and former veterinarian. But Jack admitted he was reluctant to make the visit. "What if the doctor has a flashback to his former career, and I come home neutered?" Jack joked.

Dr. Gaver put Jack through a battery of tests. "The MRI resulted in some good news and some bad," said Jack. "The good news is that there was no sign of a brain tumor. The bad news—there was no sign of a brain, either."

All blood tests came back normal, and Jack was quickly dubbed the poster boy for heart health. Thirteen months passed without further fainting spells. Then, on January 21, 2003, the familiar feeling returned. "Spinning like a seasick seal, my head hit the desk with a thump."

The following day while Jack's wife, Karen, and friends were at a restaurant, Jack's head hit the desk again. After the third hit, Jack heard someone call out 911, and he knew he was "not playing Bingo in St. Jerome's church basement."

The EMTs arrived, and soon after Jack was in the emergency room going through another battery of tests. Dr. Hill, the physician on call, was aptly named, according to Jack. "I was already over the hill," said Jack, "and appeared well on my way to under the hill until the good doctor stabilized me."

Jack doesn't remember the ambulance ride to St. Luke's Hospital in Milwaukee, Wisconsin, but "I felt the aftershock a month later when I received the bill. Thirty dollars a mile isn't bad if you're traveling the gold streets of glory, but it seemed excessive for I-94! Fortis Insurance Company agreed. They paid only half of the charges, though they failed to explain which half of the trip was, in their view, 'medically unnecessary.'"

Meanwhile, Jack remained "the mystery man of the cardiac unit." Dr. Berger, a specialist, even presented Jack's case at a symposium for cardiologists. Three days after another exam, Jack was granted a permanent pass to go home.

No driving for awhile, but no problem. "Fresh air and homeward bound," said Jack, "was more than a trade-off. Experiencing the Kettle Moraine landscape clothed in its brilliant white winter regalia was all the therapy I needed at the moment," said Jack. And of course his family and the collection of four-legged friends that welcomed him onto their property did more for his recovery than any prescription or medical contraption.

Jack said he knew the Lord had kept him alive for a purpose. God hadn't yet finished his work in Jack's life, and he didn't trust anyone else to do it for him. Good thing for Jack's sons, too. They'd have been bummed big time if they'd lost their "gold series" Packer tickets—which their dad provided each year.

Reflection

Above all else, guard your heart, for it is the wellspring of life (Proverbs 4:23).

Talking to God

What an interesting verse, dear God, one to take 'to heart' (pun intended)! You tell me clearly to take care of myself so I can live a long and healthy life praising you and telling others of your marvelous works in creation and in me.

Love and Marriage

Say It Again, Sam!

Carl, aged 81, had his eye on Darlene, aged 79. The two had met at a dance for seniors one week and had been seeing each other ever since—rather, *trying* to see each other.

Both were a bit hard-of-hearing, but that was okay. They could sympathize with one another over their mutual lack. Carl invited Darlene to lunch one afternoon in the city. "Meet you at Fifth and Forty-ninth at one o'clock," he shouted into the telephone.

"Fine by me," said Darlene. "I'll take the early afternoon bus and see you then."

The following day Darlene boarded the bus at the corner near her apartment house and enjoyed the ride, excited about her date with the handsome Carl. She even allowed her mind to wander into the future. Maybe they'd be married someday—soon—she hoped since at their ages, time was truly running out.

Darlene stepped down from the bus when it arrived at her destination. No Carl. She waited and waited. Then she took out the paper she'd used to scribble the time and place. Sure enough. She got it right. By one-thirty she began to worry that something terrible had happened to Carl. By one-forty-five she was in a huff. She'd been stood up! *The nerve of him,* she thought. *It's not as though he is a young buck with women lined up down the block just to spend an afternoon with him.*

Darlene caught the next bus home. As she walked in the door, the phone rang. It was Carl. She didn't know whether to listen to him or hang up.

"Where were you?" he asked. "I waited and waited."

"Where were *you?*" Darlene shouted. "*I* waited."

"I was there—right where I said I'd be," said Carl. "Fifth and Forty-ninth at one o'clock."

Darlene felt her face grow warm with embarrassment. "I was at *Sixth* and Forty-ninth at one o'clock," she replied, "just as I thought you said."

They both laughed and set a new date—to shop for hearing aids!

Reflection

Like an earring of gold or an ornament of fine gold is a wise man's rebuke to a listening ear (Proverbs 25:12).

Talking to God

Lord, I need a rebuke now and again. I think I know what I'm doing. I think I hear what I need to get. I think I'm on target, only to find out I missed by a wide margin. Whew! What a lesson in humility. Keep me on track, O Lord, and do not let my pride get in the way of hearing and doing your Word.

Heartthrob

My sweet mother died in October 2003, at the age of 89. Shortly after she passed on, my sister June handed over some of Mom's diary entries in a book I had given her as a gift on Mother's Day some years before.

I always knew Mom loved our father, and he loved her with equal passion. Everyone who saw them together was aware of their special relationship. Mom was also known for her dry wit and ready humor on all occasions. So I was not surprised to see the two combined in one of her writings in 1992 dedicated to her husband, Phil, my father.

> To Phil:
>
> To hit my target heart rate, I can exercise vigorously for twenty minutes—OR—I can sit around and think of you.

Reflection

May the Lord make your love increase and overflow for each other and for everyone else (1 Thessalonians 3:12).

Talking to God

Lord, you are my heartthrob, my ever-present companion, my first love. Help me to give to others—my family, friends, even strangers—out of the abundance of your love for me. It is good to have the love of a spouse, but it's even better to have the love of the God of the universe.

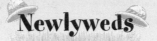

Newlyweds

Joyce hugged each of her daughters and then her new sons. "Bye. Drive safely," she called as they settled into their vehicles, buckled up, and headed home.

"Love you," she shouted after them, realizing they probably couldn't hear her. That was okay. She continued waving till both cars had rounded the curve and were out of sight.

Joyce returned to the house and noticed how quiet it was, a contrast to the good noise that had filled the rooms during her children's visit. She walked around turning off lights and collecting coffee cups and glasses that had been left behind in various rooms. She gathered up the used napkins and tossed them into the trash and stacked the dirty dishes.

Her grown daughters had come home for the weekend with their new husbands—Joyce's sons-in-law—a term she'd have to get used to. She liked both the men. In fact she loved them, but it still seemed odd that they were actually part of her family.

It was too early to go to bed. The news didn't hold Joyce's attention, and she couldn't settle down to read. Her mind was reeling with conversations and memories of the visit.

She wandered into the bathroom at the end of the hall and collected the towels, remembering how often she had done that for her daughters when they lived at home. Over the weekend each of her daughters and their new husbands stayed in the girls' old rooms. It felt odd to Joyce not to be able to walk in at any time and sit on their beds to talk. She wondered if they missed her as much as she missed them.

Joyce stripped the sheets off the bed in Katie's room and pulled the blankets back up, smoothing them into place till she had a chance to remake the bed. She tossed the linens on the washing machine and trotted down the hall to Heather's old room.

A moment later Joyce burst out laughing. She had expected things to change somewhat now that her daughters were married, but here was something she had not considered. As she pulled back the bedding from Heather's bed, she found, tucked in the bottom of the sheets, a pair of boxer shorts that obviously had been shed in a hurry!

Remembering the fun and pleasure she and her beloved Scott had enjoyed as newlyweds, Joyce laughed till the tears ran down her cheeks. Apparently Heather and her husband had enjoyed their weekend. She couldn't wait to tease her daughter about the lost item and watch her blush.

"This mother-in-law business is going to be more fun than I thought," she said aloud.

Reflection

The husband should fulfill his marital duty to his wife, and likewise the wife to her husband (1 Corinthians 7:3).

Talking to God

Lord, when I see young marrieds caught in each other's gaze, filled with hope for the future and eager for the joy and pleasure of marital love, I am reminded of that season in my life. I, too, had stars in my eyes. Today, however, my gaze has broadened and deepened. I know that you, and you alone, are my one true love and will be so for all eternity, regardless of what happens here on earth.

The Honeymooners

My husband stood in the lobby of the Wyndham Hotel in San Diego, California, ready for a day's work—ushering convention-goers into the correct limo or bus to be chauffeured to the airport. As men and women poured out of the elevators, he held up a sign with their company's name on it, and motioned the crowd in the direction they should go.

At one point an elderly couple emerged and walked slowly toward the front door. Charles rushed over to assist them. "Are you with my group?" he asked, holding up his sign so they could read it easily.

"No, no," said the man. "We're on our honeymoon."

That response sparked Charles' interest. "Your honeymoon? How wonderful. Congratulations!" he said, smiling broadly. "Where are you going?"

"We're visiting our four grown children," said the man. "She has two, and I have two."

"How nice of you to spend your honeymoon with your kids," said Charles. "I hope they appreciate it."

"They certainly do," said the gentleman. "You see our trip got a bit delayed. We were married last January, and here it is November and we're just now ready to go. My wife, here," he added, touching her arm fondly, "got so excited about our marriage that she broke her hip the day after the wedding! We've had to stay put ever since," he added and laughed out loud.

Charles joined him. It was pretty funny in a weird sort of way. The man and woman bantered back and forth as Charles took in every word. The woman playfully accused her husband of exaggerating, and then reminded him that on their wedding night he had misplaced his hearing aid, and they spent half the night looking for it. "Now you tell me," she said, looking at Charles, "who you think was the most excited."

"I'm not going to touch that one," said Charles, backing away playfully.

"Tell me, how did you meet?" my husband asked, eager for more details.

"In an assisted living facility," she said. "We were sitting at the same dinner table one night."

"How nice that you found one another!" Charles added.

"I'm sure happy," said the man, "though I'm not sure what's in store for me. You see," he said, cupping his hands around his mouth as if to guard a secret, "I married an older woman."

His wife poked him in the ribs with her elbow but that didn't stop him.

"She's 84," he said, for all to hear, "and I'm only 81!"

He redeemed himself fast before she bopped him over the head with her handbag.

"We might be in our 80s," he said whimsically, "but we're the two luckiest kids on the block."

Charles had to agree.

Reflection

For this reason a man will leave his father and mother and be united to his wife, and the two will become one flesh (Ephesians 5:31).

Talking to God

Dear Lord, what a charming story. I love knowing that people can still find a loving relationship even when time seems to be running out. You bring men and women together in marriage to comfort and please, to help and to enjoy one another. Thank you, God, that you care about your people, and you give each one what is right according to your perfect will.

Weak in the Knees

When my first husband's mother died, his dad was lost. John and Betty had been companions, friends, parents, and partners for nearly 50 years. We all expected him to curl up in his favorite armchair and watch television till the Lord took him home. But he surprised us all. About a year after Betty died, John not only got out of his chair, but he sold the family house, packed up what he wanted and needed, and moved to Minneapolis where he had been born and raised.

Suddenly he was a man with a mission. He was about to go a-courtin'! He remembered a certain young lady named Gertrude, whom he had known and visited with during his youth. He took the initiative to inquire about her—some 50 years after he had last seen her. At this point he didn't know whether or not she was still alive.

He persisted in his search until he got the news he was looking for—she was alive, well, single (her husband had passed away), and living alone in an apartment not far from where he now lived. John told us later that it took all the nerve he had to pick up the phone, dial the number, and then hope she'd not only answer it, but remember who he was.

The desire of his heart came true. She not only remembered him from 50 years before, but she remembered him well! And she was delighted to hear from him.

John invited Gertrude to join him for dinner.

"Of course. Name the time and I'll be ready," she said.

"Wednesday. Six P.M.," he replied. "I'll be there with bells on." He knew he sounded a bit corny, but she chuckled so he supposed it was all right with her. He hadn't been on the "dating scene" for over half a century. He knew he was out of touch with what to say to a "young lady" he hoped to win over.

John talked often of that reunion with Gertrude. "I got out of my car," he said, "took big gulps of fresh air, cleared my throat a hundred times, then practiced what I'd say when she opened the door."

But nothing went as John had rehearsed. He began walking up the steps to her second-floor apartment and apparently she heard him coming because the door swung open as he stepped out onto the landing. "I couldn't say a word," he later reported. "I was speechless. My knees started knocking. I was 15 and in love all over again."

John and Gertrude married four months later. They spent their honeymoon in Hawaii—a place John had always dreamed of visiting. They returned to Minneapolis, bought a condominium, and decorated it to suit their taste.

Four years later John died of emphysema. I called Gert to express my sympathy and to thank her for taking such good care of our dear John, whom we all loved so much.

"There was no one like John," she commented, with a smile in her voice. "We didn't have much time together, but the time we did have was worth the 50-year wait!"

And then she summed up her love and affection for her late husband with these words: "I'd rather have lived in a tent with John than in a palace with anyone else."

Reflection

Enjoy life with your wife, whom you love (Ecclesiastes 9:9).

Talking to God

Lord, it is a joy to know that age is no barrier to love and friendship and marriage. When we walk with you in trust and faith, nothing is impossible. Your gifts are boundless, and your love never ending.

New Every Morning

Lonnie could hardly wait to show her husband the walking path she'd discovered not far from home. Lined with trees and song birds, it ran between two lakes. The beauty and solitude provided a pleasant escape from the noise and busyness of suburbia.

One day they stole away for a walk. This was Lonnie's opportunity to take Ray to her new spot. When they arrived, Ray looked around. He didn't appear impressed with the beauty or uniqueness of the setting.

"We've been here before," he said.

Lonnie was disappointed. That wasn't the reaction she'd hoped for.

"No, we haven't," she protested.

"Yes, we have," he insisted. "We biked here a couple of years ago."

Lonnie strained to remember. Finally she laughed it off.

"Well, there's one advantage to forgetfulness," she said with a smile. "Every day is fresh, and every experience is new. God does cause all things to work together for good, doesn't he?"

Lonnie and Ray linked hands and went for a walk on their "new" path.

Reflection

You have made known to me the path of life; you will fill me with joy in your presence, with eternal pleasures at your right hand (Psalm 16:11).

Talking to God

Lord, when I get up with the birds, pull on my duds, and pound my way around the block or through the park, I feel energized. It's a great way to start my day! Why don't I make a habit of it then? I give in to small excuses. I'm tired. I have urgent business. I had a bad night. It's cloudy and gray. Help me, Lord, to overcome my reasons and to focus instead on the benefit—the joy of your presence under the sky and sun you created for me.

Close Call in Paris!

Margaret K. and her husband, Martin, flew to Paris for a romantic getaway. Their kids were grown and out of the house, and Martin was nearing retirement. It was the perfect time to enjoy such a holiday.

One afternoon as they strolled hand-in-hand toward the Eiffel Tower, Margaret remarked on how warm it was. She asked Martin if he was too hot in the nylon jogging outfit he was wearing.

"How about tying your jacket around your waist?" she suggested, indicating that she had done the same thing with hers.

"Good idea," he said and followed her example.

A moment later, as they approached the tower, Martin stopped cold, a look of shock on his face.

"What's the matter?" Margaret asked, alarmed.

Martin looked down, then burst out laughing. His worst fear had not come true after all. He had felt a funny sensation at his feet and feared that his pants had burst open and slid down his legs. Not so. It was only the nylon jacket that had shimmied down to his ankles.

"We laughed till our sides ached," said Margaret.

Reflection

A time to weep and a time to laugh (Ecclesiastes 3:4).

Talking to God

Lord, one of the great joys of being married is laughing together—especially over little things. There are so many details to smile about each day. Sometimes, though, I overlook them because I'm in a hurry or I'm too serious or I'm in a grumpy mood. Please help me to remember there is a "time to laugh" and to enjoy it—with my spouse.

I Heard You the First Time

Barbara Jean's husband, Vic, is a man who takes his time about everything. He cannot be hurried. Period. "Sometimes it takes two weeks for him to get back to me with an answer to a question," said Barbara Jean (B.J.). "By then I've forgotten what I asked!" For example, the couple moved to La Jolla, California, because of Vic's work assignment. After three years he wanted to retire early, even though they were not what B.J. thought of as financially secure.

One night B.J. posed the question, "Vic, would you like to move back to D.C.? Now that you're retired, there's nothing to hold us here."

No response.

B.J. asked the question again, a little louder this time. She admits she likes instant answers. "Even wrong ones will do," she said, "as long as he says *something.*"

Two weeks later Vic walked in after playing a round of golf with some buddies.

"I've decided," he said with conviction.

"Decided what?" B.J. wondered aloud. She didn't have a clue as to what he was talking about.

"To stay in La Jolla," he said as though they were still having the same conversation she had initiated two weeks before.

"Today when we were playing golf at Torrey Pines, there were two 'snow birds' from the East Coast who come to California twice a year to play golf," he added. "I realized I can play twice a week for practically nothing."

"End of discussion," B.J. reported later. "And here we are 34 years later."

Reflection

He who answers before listening—that is his folly and his shame (Proverbs 18:13).

Talking to God

This story really tickles me, dear God. Ah! There is another married person on the planet besides me who wants a response—even a wrong one—as long as it involves words being spoken out loud! On the other hand, I can't change my mate. You made each of us unique and for your own purpose. So please help me to keep that in mind when our communication breaks down. Remind me to trust you to bring about the perfect answer in due time.

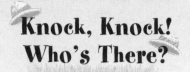

Knock, Knock! Who's There?

For Jeanne W.'s seventy-fifth birthday, her husband Jerry took her to Palm Springs for a romantic weekend. At midnight, after a lovely dinner and evening together, they returned to their motel suite.

Jerry was in a hurry to get to the bathroom, so he rushed ahead of her. As soon as he opened the exterior door to their rooms, he ran in so fast he didn't realize the door had slammed shut before Jeanne could enter. There she stood in the hall without a key!

She waited a few minutes for him to finish in the bathroom, then knocked softly so as not to awaken neighboring guests. No success. Jerry did not answer. Jeanne became concerned. Had he keeled over? Was he stuck in the bathroom? What was going on?

"Jerry," she called, "please let me in!"

Still no response.

Two men walked by with curious expressions on their faces as Jeanne glanced their way. "I could imagine what they were thinking," she said. "'Well, he must have tossed the old gal out!'"

Finally Jeanne gave up trying to raise her husband. She walked outside the building and through a maze of paths that led to the office. She was so bewildered by then she had forgotten their room number. A sympathetic desk clerk gave her the information she needed so she could phone Jerry in the room.

A sleepy voice responded to the ring. She knew her husband must have gone to bed. That only increased her ire. The nerve of him!

"Where did you say you are?" he asked. Then he followed up with the question he never should have uttered. "And why are you *there?*" he queried.

"Later he was very sorry he asked," said Jeanne.

Reflection

Husbands, in the same way be considerate as you live with your wives, and treat them with respect (1 Peter 3:7).

Talking to God

Dear God, we sure can get ourselves into trouble with our spouses—the last people we want to offend or dismiss. I feel sorry about my thoughtless remarks and careless actions. I will apologize right now. Then I know things will be right between you and me, as well.

You Need What?

Joanne walked into the senior center, a survey sheet from the Senior Social Services Agency in one hand, and a pen in the other. She was ready for her assignment.

"Talk with people," her supervisor had advised. "Spend a moment or two with each one. Find out what they're interested in, their age, if they'll share it, and any specific needs they have now that they're 65 or more. That will help us evaluate our services and make adjustments."

Joanne approached a table where four people were engaged in a game of Scribbage. An elderly woman sat to the side, watching the game, but not participating. *My first prospect,* Joanne thought. *Maybe she'll take a few minutes to talk with me.*

"Excuse me, ma'am," Joanne said. "I'm a representative from the Senior Social Services Agency in town. I wonder if you'd be willing to participate in a simple survey. We are eager to find out more about the needs of our city's seniors so we can better serve you. My name is Joanne," she added, as she stuck out her hand in a welcoming gesture.

"I'm Inez," said the woman. "Sure. Fire away."

The two women pulled their chairs away from the game-players and focused on the survey. Joanne looked at Inez and posed her first question.

"What do you consider your most critical need at this stage of your life?" Joanne asked, leaning forward, pen poised for the answer.

"A boyfriend!" said Inez.

Joanne was taken aback. That wasn't exactly the response she had expected.

She didn't want to insult Inez by telling her that romantic needs weren't part of the survey.

"Well, let's talk about that," she stammered. "Uh, what kind of man? I mean what are you looking for in a boyfriend?" Joanne asked.

"Only one requirement," said Inez with confidence. "He needs to be *functional!*"

Reflection

Be still before the LORD and wait patiently for him (Psalm 37:7).

Talking to God

Dear God, is this what it comes down to in old age? We'll settle for the most basic qualification in another human being—functionality! I want more than that in my partner. But maybe I won't have a choice. I don't know what the future holds for us. Maybe our roles will reverse. The strong will become weak and the weak strong. I won't focus on that now. I will trust that with you at our side, all will be well no matter what.

Perfectly Straight

Dick and Donna sat down to plan their family's Christmas celebration. Their four children were grown and married with kids of their own, and Dick and Donna looked forward to having everyone gather at their house for an old-fashioned get-together. They would serve Dick's famous lasagna; Donna's annual holiday salad with pears, walnuts, and cranberries; hot garlic bread; and for dessert great-grandma's butter toffee; frosted cookies; and eggnog.

Dick also planned to introduce his grandchildren to a Christmas tradition from his childhood. Everyone would gather in a circle on the floor. He'd pass an empty jar with one hand and a bag of jelly beans with the other. He'd ask each one, young and old alike, to say one thing about the current year for which they were thankful, and drop a jelly bean into the jar as they did. The jelly beans made the activity more fun. After everyone took a turn, they'd hold hands and pray a prayer of thanksgiving for the past year and ask for blessings in the year ahead.

Dick rolled his eyes. "I can hardly wait!" he exclaimed. He grabbed a pen and pad and began making notes. He liked things to be neat, orderly, and well-planned. No last-minute dashing around for him.

Donna, on the other hand, preferred to wing it. She believed everything would work out. It always had, so there was no use fretting about details. They had two weeks to prepare. What was the rush? After all, they weren't as young as they used to be.

"I want things to be *perfect*," Dick said, interrupting his wife's thoughts. "It's not every year we get all 15 of us together in one place. This is going to be a Christmas we'll remember for years to come. Now about gifts…"

Dick droned on as Donna pulled out the box of tree ornaments and began unwrapping each one. She held up the little glass ball Dick had given her on their first Christmas. She read the engraved message out loud: "From Dick to Donna—forever in Christ, forever together, 1959." She wiped a tear from her eye and looked at her husband, now a balding man of 70 and she a white-haired woman of 69. Where had the years gone?

"Donna, pay attention! You're drifting again. Let's get down to business. No daydreaming. We have only two weeks to pull all this together. Did you order the new pillows for the guest room? And what about the tablecloth and napkins—the ones with the holly berries?"

Donna stood up. She saluted and clicked her heels. "Aye, aye, sir," she said with mock solemnity, stifling a smile with a hand over her mouth. "All taken care of, sir!"

"You have that look in your eye," Dick said. "The one you've been giving me for the past 40-plus years. You ought to know me by now. I like to get a jump on things. It's too easy to mess up when you wait till the last minute. And at our age we can't take any chances. We're already forgetting things."

"I think you mean *I'm* forgetting things, don't you?"

Donna's eyes twinkled. Dick had acted concerned when she forgot a dental appointment the week before. This was her chance to tease him—something she loved to do, especially when he went into serious mode. He was just about there right now!

"Look, darling," she cooed, "it's Christmastime. Let's be partners, have fun, help each other. I don't want to feel as if I'm a private and you're the sarge barking orders."

Dick reached across the table and grabbed her hands. "You're right," he said. "Now, let's get going on the invitations and our Christmas cards. If we focus, we can go through the stack in record time and get them into today's mail. What do you say?"

Donna mumbled under her breath, *Not a thing!* This man couldn't do life any other way but according to the book. But she loved him. He was her mate, the one God gave her. So she sat down, picked up the cards, and began filling them out. She signed her name, then passed each one to Dick for his signature.

He then rolled out the stamps and began pressing them in place, one after another, until the entire pile was complete. He sat back and breathed a sigh of relief. "Now," he said, obviously proud of himself, "look at what we can accomplish when we work together as a team."

Donna smiled and picked up the stack of envelopes. She thumbed through them to be sure he hadn't missed a stamp. She let out a whoop. "D-i-c-k..." she said, drawing out his name like a Southern belle. Then she pointed to the left-hand corner of each envelope. There were the stamps...that should have been placed in the right-hand corners—the spot where people had been putting stamps ever since the postal service began. Talk about drifting!

Dick looked down, cleared his throat, and paused. His face turned red—but not for long. He managed to rescue himself with one sentence. "You can say whatever you like, but you have to admit, each stamp is *perfectly* straight!"

Donna patted his hand. "You're perfectly right, dear. They are. How about a glass of lemonade to cool us off while we restamp each envelope?"

Reflection

The wisdom of the prudent is to give thought to their ways... (Proverbs 14:8).

Talking to God

Dear Lord, marriage is such a mix of laughter, sadness, joy, and frustration—and a lot of silly behaviors too...especially as we grow older. "How did I do that?" we ask when we realize we've done something foolish. And if we don't question ourselves, our spouses will: "You did what?" Fortunately, a good laugh and plenty of forgiveness goes a long way to smooth the rough spots. Help me today to love my mate with a full heart, regardless of the quirks, and to trust that he or she will love me back!

Pet
Parade

Dog Daze!

I want a dog," I told my husband, Charles, one November night as we plopped in front of the TV.

He looked at me with a puzzled expression. "A dog?" he asked. "Since when? I thought we agreed we're too old for cats and dogs. At this stage of our life," he pontificated, "a dog could very well outlive us. That wouldn't be fair. Besides…"

"*Us?*" I said emphatically. "You, maybe, but not me. *I'm* only 60, remember?" I added, reminding him that he was a full decade older than me.

Charles paused for a moment. "I'm totally surprised," he said. "I thought the subject was closed. A dog wouldn't work in our condo. A dog needs space, a place to romp and run. And pets are expensive and time-consuming. We've been over this before, and I…"

"True," I said, remembering the reasons we had listed when I had last said I wanted a dog.

No yard.

Carpeted floors.

Vet bills.

Food.

Housebreaking.

Daily walks.

Training.

Shots.

The kennel when we're gone.

The list went on.

"I guess I'm feeling sentimental," I said. "I want something cute and cuddly to curl up with on the sofa, like when I was a kid."

Charles looked hurt. "You told me I'm cute," he said, pouting. Then he brightened. "And I love to cuddle," he added and pulled me close.

I sat up straight. "I don't think you're listening," I whined. "I want...you know, a furry little creature who..."

"I was about to volunteer again," Charles said with a wry smile. "But when you said the word 'furry', well, sorry, I can't help you there," he added as he opened his shirt and pointed to the three hairs on his chest.

"Very funny!" I said. "You know what I mean. I'm serious. I want a dog."

"Give me some time to get used to the idea," said Charles.

"Really?"

"Really!"

We laughed, hugged, and tabled the discussion—temporarily.

Six weeks later on Christmas Eve, Charles walked into the den with a huge gift box.

"For me?" I asked.

He nodded yes.

I tore into the wrappings like an excited child. I couldn't imagine what it was. We had agreed to put our gift-giving on hold that year and use the money toward new furniture.

"Charles, now I feel embarrassed," I said. "I didn't get you a gift...we promised, remember?"

"This is for both of us," he said, smiling like a ten-year-old kid.

I pulled away the snow-white tissue. And there, nestled in the center of the box, were two of the cutest and cuddliest stuffed toy dogs I'd ever seen. I burst out crying. "Oh, Charles, they're wonderful," I said, leaping into his lap and covering his face with kisses.

"Down, girl!" he joked. "You said you wanted a dog, didn't you? Well, I decided I wanted one, too. So here they are. They're small, neat, and very obedient. And they're, well, cute and cuddly and furry, too. Everything you asked for."

I pulled the dogs close and nuzzled my face into their soft fur. Each one wore a tag with a name. I plopped Dotty on my lap, and Charles grabbed Bruno. We relaxed on our favorite sofa with our two new dogs resting comfortably on our chests.

That night I placed a soft towel in a little basket, laid the dogs on top, and put the basket at the foot of our bed. They remained there without a whimper until we took them out the next morning.

I was totally content. I had my dog at last—two of them, in fact—and more than I had asked for.

Two months later, as I walked in from a business trip, I ran into our bedroom to greet the dogs as I usually did whenever I returned home. I had missed them so. But something was different this time. Two tiny heads hung over the rim of the basket.

"What's going on?" I asked Charles.

"Take a look," he said with a mischievous grin.

I lifted up the big dogs and underneath were two adorable puppies, Doby—who was dark like Bruno—and Bones—who resembled Dotty with his sad eyes and droopy ears.

"They're precious," I squealed. "How did they get here?"

"It just happened," said Charles with a twinkle in his eye. "I guess Dotty and Bruno were alone in that basket a little too long!"

Reflection

Delight yourself in the LORD and he will give you the desires of your heart (Psalm 37:4).

Talking to God

Dear Lord, thank you that having fun and being silly adds many playful moments to our lives. They bring out the childlike part of us—something we treasure even more now that we're getting older. I love knowing that you take delight in your children—regardless of our ages—and that you enjoy my laughter as much as you empathize with my tears.

Mysterious Kitty

Marilyn heard a faint sound like a soft meowing. She looked outside the window of her room in the convalescent home where she lives, but she didn't see anything. One of the nurses stopped by and heard the same "meow, meow, meow." She didn't see any signs of a cat, either.

Soon the little cries grew louder—even desperate. Marilyn again looked outside, but still no signs of a cat. The sounds became so loud, Marilyn knew the little thing—wherever it might be—needed help.

She asked the nurse to request that the maintenance man check the roof, and she asked one of the housekeepers to listen, as well. Neither of them heard a peep. Marilyn was beginning to panic. She wanted to help, but how could she if she couldn't find the kitten?

Marilyn then engaged a series of other personnel to take a look. First one of the employees from Central Service, then the Director of Nursing. "By this time, I was nearly in tears," said Marilyn. "The sound had persisted for more than an hour."

Marilyn said she knew the kitty was crying desperately. Someone had to do something.

"Are you sure you aren't hallucinating?" asked the director.

Marilyn was appalled at the question, but she responded calmly. "No, I am not hallucinating. There is a cat on the roof crying desperately."

The woman left, appearing disgruntled, and finally one of the nurses told Marilyn that the charge nurse would call the animal shelter to rescue the cat. It seems Marilyn's neighbor had heard the same meowing the night before.

"I was really relieved!" said Marilyn.

But there was a problem. Someone from the shelter could not come until the following day.

"A lot of help that was," Marilyn said. "I knew I'd have to endure the kitten's pathetic cries for another night."

Then Marilyn's aide walked into her room, and all of a sudden they both heard, "Meow, meow, meow" louder than before. Finally, she had proof! A cat was in trouble.

Suddenly the nurse's aide had an idea. "Are you sure the kitten isn't in the room?" she asked.

"Immediately she began looking behind the furniture near my bed," said Marilyn. "And there she found a tiny kitten scrunched up behind my dresser—and the poor little thing couldn't get free."

Just then Marilyn's friend—who happened to be a cat lover—phoned Marilyn. When she heard the story of the mysterious kitty she told Marilyn it was probably looking for its mother.

She suggested putting some food out so they could get her to stop darting around in fright. When she relaxed they could then pick her up. No one ever figured out how the little critter made it into the nursing home, walked into Marilyn's room, and got trapped behind her dresser!

Someone had said there was a larger cat on the grounds so if they put the kitty outside, her mother would hear the meowing and come and get her.

So much for the story of the mysterious kitten who, even though only a baby, landed in a convalescent home!

Reflection

Rescue the weak and needy; deliver them from the hand of the wicked (Psalm 82:4).

Talking to God

Dear God, thank you for the gift of cats and dogs and kittens and puppies. They are so dependent on their human friends. You say in your Word that when we care for the least of your creatures we are caring for you. May I remember that about all those who come into my life who are less fortunate than I am.

My, How You've Changed!

Mary Beth observed her sister-in-law showing pictures of herself when she was young to her granddaughter, Audrey. The two enjoyed leafing through the album that displayed Grandma from birth to adulthood.

As they closed the album, Audrey's grandma looked at her to see what comment, if any, she had about seeing her as a child and teen. It's hard for little kids to imagine that adults were ever children themselves.

Audrey looked up then turned to her grandmother with a quizzical expression. "Grandma, whatever happened to your face?"

Reflection

Charm is deceptive, and beauty is fleeting; but a woman who fears the LORD is to be praised (Proverbs 31:30).

Talking to God

Lord, I'm aware of how quickly my face is changing. I thought it would be years and years before I looked like my grandparents, but here I am—an older person myself—with wrinkles and loose skin of my own. It seems only yesterday that it was firm and smooth. I'm so relieved to know that you have your eye on the part of me that really matters—the condition and appearance of my soul.

Hair-Raising Tale

B.J.'s granddaughters have thick, shiny, light-brown hair—enough for more than two children. B.J. couldn't help but be jealous, especially when she and the girls played "beauty parlor," one day. Just for fun, they experimented with their grandma's antiquated hair curlers.

B.J.'s hair is short, thin, and gray, so there wasn't much they could do with hers. She admitted she was relieved that Nicole and her sister, Mandy, age three, had not inherited her "hair" genes.

"I wish I could have just half of your long beautiful tresses," B.J. said with a touch of envy.

"But, Mema," five-year-old Nicole said matter-of-factly, "God made you the way He wanted *you* to be! You should be happy."

B.J. smiled. That timely and touching comment raised the hair on her arms!

Reflection

Your beauty should not come from outward adornment, such as braided hair and the wearing of gold jewelry and fine clothes (1 Peter 3:3).

Talking to God

I know what your Word says about not making too much of our hair, but Lord, sometimes it's hard not to envy the thick, shiny tresses of younger people. I had hair like that once. Remember? Now I'm experimenting with how to give what's left a fuller look, to hide the thinning spots, to give it some oomph! Please don't think me vain, dear God. I'm just an older person trying to look my best.

Only One Thing Missing!

One day when Jean had a few private moments with her six-year-old granddaughter, she noticed the little girl studying Jean's face, her hair, her figure! Jean had gray hair and some wrinkles at the time and, as she admits, "I still have them."

"Grandma," her granddaughter said, "you know, you look just like a teenager—except for your head!"

Oh, oh! Time for dark glasses and a big hat!

Reflection

Even when I am old and gray, do not forsake me, O God, till I declare your power to the next generation, your might to all who are to come (Psalm 71:18).

Talking to God

Has it come to that, dear Lord? Our grandkids have to keep us up on what we look like—as if we're in doubt! Don't I wish? No, it's all too clear, I'm older and my face tells it all. I just have to keep reminding myself that a pretty hat can do wonders. And it's probably time for a new pair of sun specs too.

Homework Rebate

Angie is a coupon clipper. She admits she loves a rebate when she can find one—especially if the coupon is redeemable at the store instead of by mail.

One time when her grandson Michael was in third grade, she realized her penchant for a good deal had influenced him. She took care of him after school that year while his parents worked. "I liked him to do his homework before his mother and father picked him up," said Angie, "so they wouldn't have so much to handle when they got home."

While checking Michael's work one afternoon, Angie noticed that he had not put the current date on any of his papers. He post-dated every one! She asked him about this odd practice, and he had a ready response.

"I don't want them to expire," he said.

Reflection

All your sons will be taught by the LORD, and great will be your children's peace (Isaiah 54:13).

Talking to God

Lord, thank you for the opportunity to be part of my grandchildren's education—whether formal or informal. I know that whenever we're together they are looking at me and listening to me in a way my own children never did! I think that's a good thing. They seem to love me just as I am and want to learn from me. Wow! That's quite a responsibility. Let me always show them who you are by example and by the words I speak.

Feliz Navidad

Wendy and her family gathered at her parents' home in Connecticut for their annual Christmas gathering. She and her husband, her brother and his son, Wendy's daughter and her husband and son, had all come to share the gracious hospitality of Wendy's 82-year-old mother and 88-year-old father.

The elderly couple were limited in what they could do physically with their great-grandson, Kyle, but they enjoyed talking with him and discovering what a mature little boy he was for someone of only six years of age.

Kyle probably sensed that he had a willing audience so he chose to demonstrate his command of some Spanish words, which he had recently learned in kindergarten. He turned to Great Grandpa and said in a melodic voice with just the right accent, "Feliz Navidad, GG-Pa."

A look of horror and disbelief crossed his great-grandfather's face.

"What do you mean, there is no God!" the old man exclaimed while cupping his left ear in his hand and leaning over to confront his blasphemous and bewildered great-grandson.

Kyle repeated more firmly, "Feliz Navidad, GG-Pa."

Wendy's father looked around with disbelief and pronounced judgment upon the children of this day who were obviously in need of some good teaching. He did not understand how this had happened to *his* great-grandson.

Amid Kyle's confused stare, GG-Pa's disgust, and everyone else's laughter, his adult children suddenly realized that their father was reacting to what he *thought* he heard!

Reflection

For the LORD gives wisdom, and from his mouth come knowledge and understanding (Proverbs 2:6).

Talking to God

Lord, I'm wondering if maybe I do the same thing as GG-Pa—only with you. I act, I speak, I respond according to what I think I hear you saying. This is a good reminder to ask you for wisdom so that I will not act on my own interpretation but, instead, on the knowledge and understanding you provide.

Chicken Feet Hands

When Freda's two daughters, Janet and Julie, were young, Freda had a custom of inviting two elderly sisters to lunch each year. The ladies lived out of state, so their annual get-together was a special treat for everyone. "The elder was a 'spinster,'" said Freda, "and the younger, a grandmother."

On one of their visits, Freda's daughters were quite excited about having company for lunch. They invited the elderly sisters to join them in play, such as ring-around-the-rosy.

The elder sister, the more outgoing of the two, joined right in. Julie, Freda's youngest daughter, even invited her to ride her bike—surely a sign of how welcome they were. Much to Freda's relief, the woman declined!

As they held hands during a game, Julie stared at Aunt Sally's hands. Then she blurted out, "Aunt Sally, why do your hands look like chicken feet?"

"I thought I would die of embarrassment," said Freda. "I reprimanded my very confused child, who had no idea she had insulted her elderly playmate."

116

Thankfully, Aunt Sally, came to Freda's rescue. She laughed with genuine amusement. "Why, they do look like chicken feet!" she said and kept right on playing.

"Now, *I'm* a senior," said Freda. "And the tables have been turned. Recently, while teaching the four- and five-year-olds in Sunday school, a new four-year-old girl named Hannah joined us."

"Why are you both so old?" the child asked Freda's co-teacher, who is about the same age as Freda. The woman tried to explain the aging process in terms a four-year-old could understand—not an easy thing to do.

Freda said she is now preparing for other unexpected and intrusive questions. Maybe one of them will be, "Miss Freda, why do your hands look like chicken feet?"

Reflection

He lifted me out of the slimy pit, out of the mud and mire; he set my feet on a rock and gave me a firm place to stand (Psalm 40:2).

Talking to God

Kids can really blow us away with their frank questions and surprising observations. At first I feel insulted, but then I think maybe that's just what I need at this stage of life—a good honest look at myself, chicken-feet hands and all. As long as you have given me a firm place to stand—on your love and on your Word—then what does it matter how my hands look?

Senile Santa

Cindy's three married children and their spouses were with her and her husband in Alpine, Arizona, for their first white Christmas in their new cabin.

She had hung nine stockings on the new river-rock fireplace. "Traditionally," said Cindy, "I filled the stockings each Christmas Eve and my daughter, Sarah, enjoyed filling one for me."

On this particular Christmas morning, the family opened the packages that were nestled under the tree, and then all sat down for a big breakfast.

"I glanced at the fireplace," said Cindy, "and realized that I'd totally forgotten to fill the stockings I was in charge of! My sock, however, bulged with surprises while the other eight were as flat as the pancakes we were eating."

Embarrassed, Cindy made a joke of it. She laughed and pointed to the fireplace, "Look at our Christmas stockings!" she proclaimed in front of the family. "All of you must have been naughty this year! And I must be the *only* one who's been nice!"

Without missing a beat, Cindy's 25-year-old son, David, quipped, "Either that or Santa is getting senile!"

Reflection

They will celebrate your abundant goodness and joyfully sing of your righteousness (Psalm 145:7).

Talking to God

Lord, thank you for family and friends and Christmas celebrations. They bring out the best in all of us. We laugh and joke and talk and eat. We leave feeling close to each other and closer to you as we share gifts and honor your birth.

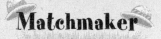

Matchmaker

Donna's 19-year-old granddaughter has learned the meaning of the term "courtship." She has decided she prefers that to dating. Her 13-year-old brother, Ethan, knowing his sister's preference, was, as Donna observed, "on the lookout for the right guy for his sister."

One evening, Ethan and his dad were working on a truck transmission with a single, good looking, 25-year-old young man. Ethan ran into the house and found his sister.

"Quick change your shirt, comb your hair, and come meet this guy," he said tugging at her sleeve.

His sister informed him that she was not interested in meeting this mechanic. Later, Ethan walked in with less enthusiasm, now that he'd had a chance to watch and listen to the young man.

"It's a good thing you didn't come out," he said with conviction, knowing his sister's standards were high. "He uses bad language—like a truck driver!"

Donna and her husband had a good laugh. Kids do say the darnedest things.

Reflection

His speech is smooth as butter, yet war is in his heart (Psalm 55:21).

Talking to God

Lord, I'm enjoying hearing my grandchildren speak up when they see or hear something that isn't right. That means they're paying attention to your teachings, to what their parents and grandparents have been reading and sharing with them. I love seeing this next generation begin to see the difference between words of truth and kindness and words of dishonesty and disrespect.

Wrinkle-Free

Sharon admits that she enjoys a good story about other women going through menopause since she's in that phase of life herself. One night her husband came home from work and shared a funny story with her.

"It seems the sister of one of his coworkers," said Sharon, "recently had some mid-life maintenance (cosmetic surgery) on her face. After church a few Sundays later, she was standing in the foyer with some relatives waiting to shake hands with the minister before leaving. Suddenly, her five-year-old nephew came up to her and said, 'Gosh, Aunt Jennie, I almost didn't recognize you without your wrinkles!'"

Reflection

See that you do not look down on one of these little ones. For I tell you that their angels in heaven always see the face of my Father in heaven (Matthew 18:10).

Talking to God

Lord, I'm trying to imagine what my transformed body will look like in heaven. Not a spot or sag or wrinkle anywhere! Will my grandchildren come

*up to me and wonder who I am? Thank you for
reminding me not to take offense at what they
say, especially when they are innocent of any
intention to hurt me. They just say what pops
into their heads. Maybe that's a good thing. I'm
grateful you don't mince words, either. I need
to hear everything you have to say to me.*

Why, Grandma? Why?

Teri and her precocious nearly four-year-old grand-daughter were sharing an afternoon together, covering a bit of family history. "Catherine, would you like to hear a story about your daddy when he was my little boy?" Teri asked.

"Sure, Grandma, tell me," she said as she settled herself on Teri's lap. Cate shifted restlessly, then pressed Teri's lips with a finger, signaling her grandma to start talking.

"When your daddy was a little boy, he loved to learn things," Teri began.

"Why?" asked Cate, copying Teri's soft storytelling voice.

"Well, he was a very curious little fellow," she answered, smiling.

"Why?" Cate asked again, as she tilted her head.

"He just wanted to know everything about everything," said Teri.

"Why?" Cate persisted, scrunching up her face.

"Well, he had a good brain, and he just wanted to know more and more."

"Why?" Cate asked again as she stretched her neck, lifted her chin and asked again, "Why?"

"Honey," Teri said, "he was just like you are *right now!* He would listen to Grandma tell him things, and he would ask for more information about whatever Grandma would say!"

"Why?" she asked yet again, as she turned up her hands, palms flat. Maybe she expected the answer to be handed over.

"That's just the way he was," said Teri, bringing the unfinished story to a conclusion.

"Why?" she countered.

By that time, Teri was feeling a bit weak! She glanced at her husband.

He snickered. "I knew she was going to say that," he stated.

Cate sat up and stared right into her grandmother's eyes. "Grandma, I said 'why?' Did you hear me?" Then she took Teri's arm and shook it. "Why, Grandma, w-wh-y-y-y? Why did Daddy do that? What did he say? Grandma, can you hear me?"

Catherine brought Teri back from her momentary reverie by putting her two little hands around Teri's face, trying to reposition it to help Teri focus on her so she could hear better.

"Gran-n-ndm-m-a-a-a-a, don't you know? Look at my face, Grandma. Can you hear me? Look at my eyes, Grandma. Why didn't Daddy know? Couldn't he talk like me? Huh, Grandma? Tel-l-l me-e-e, GRANDMA! WHY-DID-DADDY-SAY-THAT, GRANDMA?"

At this point, Grandpa, who was listening and observing this scenario from the other side of the room, was nearly choking, trying to muffle his laughter. Teri suggested they all

take a much-needed nap, as she gently led Cate toward the
bedroom.

"Why, Grandma?"

Reflection

My mouth will speak words of wisdom; the
utterance from my heart will give understanding
(Psalm 49:3).

Talking to God

*Lord, I have so many questions. "Why this and
why that?" I'm just like a curious child. I'll
bend your ear when I finally get to heaven and
can ask them all. It occurs to me, though, that
by then none of them will matter. I will be just
so happy to have made it to the place you've
prepared for me, where cares and worries, sick-
ness and fear do not exist. Then all that is
unknown to me here will be known, and I will
have full understanding and wisdom as you
promised.*

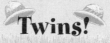

Twins!

It was Betty's birthday. And best of all, her family called to wish her a happy one. Her granddaughter Jessica got on the line and in a loving voice said, "Happy birthday, Grandma."

"Thanks, honey," Betty replied. "Today I'm 61 years old, but I've decided to turn the numbers around and be 16 instead," she added, feeling quite clever with her attempt at spontaneous humor.

"Well," Jessica shot back without hesitation. "I'm eight. If you add eight plus eight, you get 16. Hey, Grandma," she said laughing, "we're *twins!*"

Reflection

From the lips of children and infants you have ordained praise because of your enemies, to silence the foe and the avenger (Psalm 8:2).

Talking to God

I don't think much about my age anymore. One birthday tends to blend into another. As long as I feel young, I'm not really old, is the way I look at it. But I also appreciate that my grand-children want to cheer me up, helping me "seem" younger than I really am. I think I'll listen to them instead of some of the other people I know—you know the ones, Lord.

At Least One!

I'm always cold, even in Southern California where I live. So when I visit my daughter Erin and her family in Northern California, I always take along an extra sweater and jacket.

One weekend while visiting the family, my granddaughter Shevawn, four years old at the time, and I decided to go to a movie. As we were about to leave, I grabbed my sweater, then looked at her in shirt sleeves.

"Honey, bring a jacket or sweatshirt. It's chilly outside."

"I don't need one," she said confidently. "I'm always hot."

My daughter nodded, confirming that she was right.

"Well, I'm always cold," I said, "so I guess I'm judging by my own comfort zone. I'm getting older, and I just don't have as many hormones as I used to."

Shevawn looked at me with a puzzled expression. "What are hormones?" she asked.

I was at a loss to explain in terms a four-year-old could understand so I simply said, "Something in our bloodstream that helps control how our bodies react to certain things—like heat and cold." I wasn't sure if that was accurate, but it sounded good enough for the moment.

We went off to the movie and had a wonderful time. I had my sweater to keep me warm, and Shevawn never complained of being cold.

The following day we decided to go to the park in the morning. The sun was shining and the air felt warm. I pulled on a turtleneck shirt but decided to leave my sweater at home.

As we walked out the door, Shevawn turned to me with a compassionate look on her face. "Grammy, don't forget your sweater," she said. "Remember, you don't have as many hormones as you used to."

"I think I'll leave it behind," I said, smiling. "But thanks for the reminder. It looks like a lovely warm day."

A smile broke across Shevawn's face as she turned to me and quipped, "Oh good, Grammy. Now you don't have to worry. I think you have at least one hormone left."

Reflection

Comfort, comfort my people, says your God (Isaiah 40:1).

Talking to God

When our grandchildren are young we take care of them. And as they grow up and I grow older, they want to take care of me. At first I balk. "I'm not that old," I think to myself. But then I realize they simply want to comfort and protect me, just as you do, Lord. They love helping me put on my sweater and giving me their favorite seat in the van. And when we go to the movies, they pass the popcorn without even being asked. I like this role. I think I'll stick with it for a few more years.

Games
Seniors Play

Mill City Laundromat

My husband, Charles, and I join a group of friends each summer for a car camp in the Sierra Mountains in Northern California. One year we were flooded out during our last night in the campground. We woke up to a wet air mattress, a leaking tent, and a down comforter saturated by the rain that trickled through a seam in the roof! So we threw everything into our car and headed out. We didn't give a hoot about organizing any of our gear. Our goal was to pack and *go!* When we hit town, we realized we couldn't drive 700 miles home with a car that was steaming up fast from the soggy bundles everywhere we looked. So we decided to stop at the Mill City Laundromat, do our wash, have a bite to eat, then head home.

We bought soap, exchanged our dollars for quarters, and began a marathon of washing—taking over four machines at once. Next we loaded up four dryers. Two hours later we had clean, dry clothes and other items, and we could be on our way.

As we packed the car we realized we were missing a few items—a blanket and a set of sheets! Oh no! They were still in the washers. I thought Charles had put them in the dryer. He thought I had. So there we were, stuck for another hour.

Once again, we finished the task and laughed it off as a senior moment—until we got in the car and discovered a bunch of wet towels under a duffel bag. They, too, needed laundering—and what about our down comforter? Should we take a chance and wash that, too, even though we'd been advised not to put down into a washing machine? *What the heck,* I thought. *It's already wet, and we can't take it home in this condition.*

Back to the Mill City Laundromat we went, armed with smelly wet towels and a drenched king-sized comforter that when wet weighs as much as my 16-year-old grandson. Two more hours passed. At last we were ready to fold the final loads and head out—only to discover the advice we had received about down comforters was accurate! It cost us five dollars in quarters to learn the truth. We had a big bulky collection of frizzed up feathers in a cotton cover. We got in the car, laughed, cried—then stopped at the nearest dumpster and tossed it!

We can hardly wait to go camping next year!

Reflection

But if we have food and clothing, we will be content with that (1 Timothy 6:8).

Talking to God

I love being in your great outdoors, O Lord. What a blessing it is to stroll through a meadow, hike in the mountains, sleep under the stars. Food seems to taste better when cooked on a grill in a forest of pines. But there's a downside, too. Coming home with dirty laundry, leftover food, and the knowledge that it's back to reality. Help me to remember that it doesn't have to be that way. I can be as content in the city as I am in the woods as long as I keep my hand in yours and my eyes on you.

One Way to
Make a Friend

Alice, at age 62, takes care of her mother, who is 86 and a victim of Alzheimer's. Alice balances this responsibility by staying active as the organist at church and teaching an occasional Sunday school class.

Alice doesn't remember having had any memory problems herself until age 59. One day someone called on the phone. The caller didn't seem to recognize Alice's voice, and Alice didn't know hers, either.

"Who's speaking?" the woman asked, perhaps concerned that she had dialed incorrectly.

"I just stood there holding the phone to my ear, my mind blank as a slate," said Alice. "I wondered what I should say. In that moment I couldn't remember my own name!"

Next thing she knew, Alice blurted out, "If you'll just give me a minute, I know I can think of it!"

The caller burst into laughter. It turns out she had the wrong number, but the two women had such a good laugh at Alice's sudden moment of forgetfulness that they continued talking. They have since become friends, and now meet occasionally for an in-person conversation over coffee.

"After that incident I worried about myself for awhile," Alice admitted. "I wondered if my mind was going. Since then, however, I've had a number of 'senior moments' and now I just laugh at them and keep going.

"I'm no longer worried about getting Alzheimer's, like my mother. Whether I do or don't doesn't matter. God has taken care of me so far, and I trust him to keep on doing so."

Reflection

If one falls down, his friend can help him up (Ecclesiastes 4:10).

Talking to God

How good it is to have friends, Lord. They are among the treasures of my life—some bright and shiny as silver and some the luster of fine gold. Both have their place. I enjoy the excitement of new people on some days, and on others, I enjoy the company of a longtime friend who knows me well and loves me anyway—as you do, my dearest friend.

Talking to Myself

"Psychologists generally agree it's healthy to talk to your-self," said Connie. "So that's my excuse for doing so! Besides, I believe it's good to get my ideas and feelings out in the open and offer myself some positive feedback. I tell myself it's beneficial."

Connie admits to talking to herself more and more—more than ever before, actually. Maybe it's because she is now a senior. And she's not referring to the age thing. She believes it has more to do with the wisdom that comes from getting older.

"It just spills out as we mature," she said. "After all, God reminds us not to hide our lights under a bushel."

Still, Connie claims that talking to herself does concern her sometimes. "I wonder if I'm getting senile. I saw this behavior in my grandfather. I hope it's not hereditary."

She remembers a time years ago when she observed her grandfather standing on the front porch of their home, scolding someone with conviction—except no one was there. Connie called out to him, "Grandpa, who are you talking to?"

"Your grandma," he replied, obviously pleased that someone asked.

"But Grandma's in the house taking a nap."

"Yes, she is," he said impudently, "but this is the only time I can get a word in edgewise."

Despite family history, Connie said she's not afraid to admit that she does talk to herself—even if some people think she's a bit loony. "I talk to myself so much that my husband, Dennis, often finds it hard to figure out whether I'm addressing him or myself.

"For example, one day he walked into the room while I was having a terrific conversation with myself. Embarrassed at being caught, I told him I was praying out loud. But over time I had to tell him the truth since, shall we say, my conversations weren't always spiritual."

Connie, a writer, explained that writers are unique individuals who need this particular way of expressing themselves. Dennis told his wife that she expressed herself "plenty," but he didn't mind if she wanted to talk to herself, too.

"That way," he said, "you're sure to get the answers you want to hear!"

Reflection

Let your conversation be always full of grace, seasoned with salt, so that you may know how to answer everyone (Colossians 4:6).

Talking to God

Even when I talk to myself I'm talking to you, O Lord, because you are always on my mind and in my heart. I pray that my conversation with you, as well as with others, will be full of grace and truth and love, and that the answers I receive or give will be in keeping with your will for me.

Clueless

On a Monday evening, Barbara took a moment to think about what she wanted to do the next day. One of the family cars was in the body shop, so she had to plan ahead if she needed to use the other one. She knew she could postpone a few errands, but she really wanted to make it to her favorite produce store, Sprouts, for what is called "Overlap Day—when the ad specials run Wednesday to Wednesday instead of the usual Wednesday to Tuesday.

"Orris, my husband, graciously offered to come home at noon that day and eat lunch with me," said Barbara. "Then I could take him back to work, run my errands, and pick him up at the end of the day."

It sounded like an ideal plan—until the couple retired for the night. "As we were getting ready for bed," she said, "we both suddenly realized it was Monday night, not Tuesday night, so the plans we had made were unnecessary." Barbara would have her car back by the time Wednesday rolled around. That meant she could go to the "Overlap Day" without inconveniencing her husband. Perfect!

The next morning, however, as they were eating breakfast, Barbara suddenly thought of something important. "I've got to check Sprouts' newspaper ad," she told Orris, "to see if there's anything I want before you leave for work. If nothing hits me, then you won't need to come home at noon as we planned."

Barbara leafed through the newspaper quickly and couldn't find the usual Wednesday ad. Then it hit her! This was *Tuesday*, not Wednesday! When would she get that straight? She felt clueless. She and her husband laughed. "Well," Barbara said to Orris, as she opened the refrigerator, "you need a lunch for today, and I need to figure out what day of the week it really is."

Reflection

The LORD upholds all those who fall and lifts up all who are bowed down. The eyes of all look to you, and you give them their food at the proper time (Psalm 145:14-15).

Talking to God

I've wondered more than once what day it is. Rushing, planning, back-tracking, searching, losing—that's a typical day for me. It's a circus around here sometimes. I need to get off the fast-track and slow down so I can focus on individual tasks one at a time—dressing, eating, sleeping, praying, cleaning, talking with family members, relaxing, having fun. Please help me to live in "kingdom" time, so I will always know what day it is because you are in charge of my calendar and my life.

Money-Back Guarantee?

Debbie loves to tell the story of her mom—a senior—who one day while visiting Knott's Berry Farm in Southern California, stopped in a gift shop to browse.

A beautiful kaleidoscope caught her attention. She held it up to the light and saw a colorful display of darling dolls that changed shapes and patterns as she turned the endpiece first one way and then another. She decided to buy it and add it to her collection.

"When Mom returned home," Debbie recalled, "she held it up to her eye to enjoy the dolls all over again, but they were gone! All she could see were various patterns of the plants outside her kitchen window. Mom picked up the phone. She was perturbed. Clearly the kaleidoscope was broken."

Debbie's mother told the clerk, "When I purchased it just a few hours ago, I saw a collection of little dolls. Now all I see are the plants in my own yard!"

The mother was about to ask if the kaleidoscope came with a money-back guarantee.

"The clerk stifled a laugh," Debbie's mother later reported, as she told Debbie what happened. "The dolls are on display in the store, ma'am," the man said in a polite, but puzzled tone.

"Mom had had a major senior moment," said Debbie, "and our family won't let her forget it. Everyone enjoys it all over again—each time she tells the story!"

Reflection

The one who is throwing you into confusion will pay the penalty, whoever he may be (Galatians 5:10).

Talking to God

Dear Lord, confusing moments are hard to admit. I feel downright stupid sometimes when I finally learn the truth. "I did that?" I ask myself. "What was I thinking?" You're much kinder to me than I am to myself. I can hear you whisper a reminder that it's okay to be human. You don't expect perfection. You only want me to love you and to run to you when I am afraid or feeling dumb.

Seeing Is Believing

One day I had a near-panic attack when I couldn't find my glasses," said Bea. "I only use them for reading, but that day I really did need them."

Bea's friend and neighbor was visiting that day, so they both looked high and low, under and on top of all surfaces, but neither of them could come up with the missing glasses.

"I emptied my purse," said Bea, "checked my pockets, looked again in every conceivable place, to no avail."

Finally she decided, "Forget it. They'll turn up eventually. We were about to leave the house when I looked in the bathroom mirror, and there they were—perched on top of my head! I didn't realize it till that moment and, funnier still, my neighbor didn't see them there, either! We laughed until we cried."

I doubt Bea or her neighbor will ever choose one another as a partner in a treasure hunt!

Reflection

Moreover, our eyes failed, looking in vain for help (Lamentations 4:17).

Talking to God

Lord, you know the saying "two heads are better than one." It's not fool-proof, though. Sometimes two people are in the same mind-set, and they can't free themselves up. So they both get lost looking for what is right under their noses or perched on top of their heads. How well I know this from experience. But when I call on your Holy Spirit for help, he's right there leading, guiding, and practically pointing to the very thing I need—whether it's my glasses or a new way of looking at things. Thank you for your Spirit, O Lord.

Soap Opera

Karen R.'s 83-year-old mother e-mailed her to describe a shopping event at Costco, a large discount warehouse. She had purchased a large bucket of laundry soap one day, but when she arrived home she realized she couldn't lift it out of the trunk of the car on her own. Her husband, Hank, couldn't help since he recently had a stroke and needed every bit of his strength just to get around their house.

"After several attempts," said Karen's mom, "I decided I would just leave it in the trunk and take out cupfuls whenever I needed to wash. When it became light enough to lift, I'd carry it into the house." This sounded like a good idea under the circumstances, but then she couldn't get the lid off. At last she managed to remove the thick strip of plastic that sealed the bucket, but still she couldn't budge the lid!

Next, Karen's mom called her neighbor Ken, but no luck there. He wasn't home. His wife, Helen, who is in her mid-seventies, offered to help. The two women were able to lift the bucket out of the trunk and then with all the might they could muster, they popped off the lid, using a screwdriver for leverage!

Karen couldn't help her mother since she lives five hours away by car. But as a life coach, Karen decided to help her mother learn something positive from this experience—hoping her mother would not pull such a stunt again...or pull one that might get her into some *real* trouble.

"I responded with some *brilliant* questions," said Karen.

1. How much did the full bucket weigh?

2. How did you get it into the car in the first place?

3. Why did you buy such a large amount anyway?

4. What did you learn from this experience?

Her mother replied with equally *brilliant* answers!

1. It weighs 32 pounds, which I can move around, but not lift out of the trunk.

2. At the store, a boy loaded it onto my cart, and another loaded it into the trunk.

3. I bought it once before, thinking it would outlast me, but lo and behold the soap is gone and I'm still here!

4. What did I learn? That I miss Hank doing the hard stuff!

Reflection

She sets about her work vigorously; her arms are strong for her tasks (Proverbs 31:17).

Talking to God

God, have you noticed how hard I make things for myself? I push and pull and twist and turn, trying to accomplish alone what would be much easier with help. The next time I am tempted to rely on my own strength, remind me, please, to ask for your help.

Signs of the Times

Jan's aging father came from the Midwest to San Diego, California, to join Jan and her family for the Christmas holidays. "Dad has lost much of his short-term memory," said Jan, "so he's fortunate to have a driver who helps him fill his day with short trips around town, to the barber shop and bank, to the airport when he travels, and to other places that make him feel comfortable." Jan commented on what a wonderful companion Paul is for her father, and that he's also a good link between her dad and his three children, who are scattered around the country.

Paul e-mailed Jan the day her father was expected to arrive. He told her how excited her father was at the prospect of a vacation in California. In fact, he was so charged up he told at least ten people in the assisted living residence where he lives that he was heading to San Diego.

"That first evening after the long trip and with family all gathered here at my house," said Jan, "Dad was tired and asked us to take him home so he could go to bed. I walked him to our guest room where he has stayed many times, showed him his clothes in the closet, and said he couldn't go home because he was staying here for a few days."

He was suddenly adamant about wanting to go home. In fact, he would not accept any reason or excuse for not doing

148

so. Finally, Jan told him he couldn't go home just yet because he was in San Diego—a long way from where he lives.

"Five minutes later," said Jan, "Dad returned to the living room, once again demanding to go home." Jan's niece took him back to his room and reminded him again he couldn't leave because he was in San Diego. He seemed to understand—but only for a minute or two. Then he made the same request again.

After the third round of the same act, Jan thought of an idea to help calm him down and also to help him remember that he was indeed, in San Diego, where he had said he wanted to visit. Jan and some of her family members printed paper signs in red and green ink that read:

Welcome to San Diego.
Earlougher Family Christmas 2003

"We taped them to the mirror in his room, in his bathroom, and throughout the house," said Jan. "The rest of the week we had no further problem until we visited some friends in their home, and took Dad with us. There were no signs in their house to remind him of where he was—so of course he wanted to go home!"

Reflection

Set up road signs; put up guideposts. Take note of the highway, the road that you take (Jeremiah 31:21).

Talking to God

Lord, thank you for putting up guideposts in my life, as well as roadblocks. I need daily reminders pointing me in the right direction and motioning me away from the highway that leads to sin. Help me to choose always to follow your path so that when my time on earth is over, I will step over the threshold into your eternal presence.

Cookie Monster

My husband and I attended a weekend conference for seniors. During lunch one day, we sat next to a couple who had been married for 51 years. As we exchanged conversation about the funny things married people do to get attention from one another (in other words, the games we play), the woman offered the following account of what has been going on in their household since the year they were married.

She began baking homemade cookies right from the start and kept her cookie jar filled with her husband's favorites—often a different kind and flavor each week. Soon he was spoiled. The jar was always full, and he could help himself whenever he wanted.

After their children grew up and left home, however, the wife went back to work as a nurse and didn't have as much time for baking as she once did when she was home most everyday.

Gradually the cookies in the jar began to diminish in number and frequency. So the husband decided to leave a "hint" whenever the supply was low. He would take the lid off the jar and leave it on the countertop. His wife would then see the jar without the lid and realize that it was time to bake!

However, she didn't like this new "game." She preferred that he *speak* to her. He preferred the wordless approach. So his wife created a little game of her own. When she saw the lid on the counter, she put it back on the cookie jar. He assumed this was the signal that the jar was refilled.

Surprise! It was empty. He took the lid off, again, and set it on the counter.

Two can play this game better than one, she decided, returning the lid to the jar.

However, they got bored after only a couple of days. He wanted cookies, and she wanted conversation. They both were losing. So they called off the game and came to an agreement. They would enjoy cookies and milk or tea and cookies *together with conversation* each evening after dinner.

Reflection

Her husband has full confidence in her and lacks nothing of value (Proverbs 31:11).

Talking to God

Lord, I look forward to my "tea time" with you each afternoon when I sit before you in prayer and enjoy the banquet of blessings you have given me. Thank you for our togetherness. I love praising you for all your good gifts of life, family, friends, health, and provision.

Lookin' Good

Too Young to Be Old

"This is one of those confessions that makes me want to look both ways before talking about it," said Peggy. "I've always laughed politely at jokes about getting older, but I never quite 'got' them, until recently."

When Peggy was in her 20s, she was "carded" regularly at restaurants and other places that sold liquor. When she pulled out her checkbook to make a purchase, cashiers would chuckle condescendingly. "Why, honey," they might say, as if playing along with the joke, "you're not old enough to have a checking account." Even when Peggy flashed her driver's license as proof, few believed her.

At 30, she was in an accident that required emergency room treatment. Peggy's mother drove her to the hospital, and even she was surprised when the nurses asked her to sign the permission form.

"My daughter is 30 years old!" her mother exclaimed.

"She doesn't look a day over 16!" someone said, covering the insult!

Then one day when Peggy was in her early 40s, a handsome young security guard walked over to her as she approached the store where she worked. They struck up a conversation and the topic of age came up.

"Casually I dropped the phrase 40-something," said Peggy, not thinking much of it at the time.

Just as quickly, the young man made something of it. "Wow," he shot back, "you're the same age as my mom!"

"Reality hit like the snap of a crocodile's jaws," quipped Peggy.

Now that she has passed the mid-century mark, Peggy happily admits her joints are holding up along with her energy level.

"I'm reluctant to confess, however, that when I hear the phrase 'gettin old ain't for wimps,' it's beginning to hit home. And when I tell my age—well, no one seems surprised anymore!"

Reflection

They will still bear fruit in old age, they will stay fresh and green (Psalm 92:14).

Talking to God

Lord, thank you for promising me that I will bear fruit even when I am old. That is so encouraging! I'm not ready to hit the rocker just yet! I have a lot to give, and when I look around, there are plenty of people—especially the young ones—who could benefit from what you have shown and taught me.

Prize-Winning Dessert

On another occasion, Ginny signed up at church for a missions trip to Guatemala. "I do not speak a word of Spanish," she said, then corrected herself. "I can say 'hola' for hello, but heaven help me if the person I speak to then thinks I'm fluent in Spanish."

During the trip, the group gathered at a remote church on a Sunday morning for the worship service and a meal. All of a sudden the Guatemalan males sitting across from Ginny stared and started to laugh.

Ginny asked the interpreter what was going on, and she replied, "I just asked them to guess how old you are. The one who comes closest to your real age gets an extra dessert!"

"To my delight," said Ginny, "they all guessed between 34 and 39. I was 53 at the time. I took the two desserts!"

Reflection

Run in such a way as to get the prize (1 Corinthians 9:24).

Talking to God

Lord, it's amazing how many people enter the race of life, then drop out without trying for the prize. You promised that all who cross the finish line will be given eternal life—the reward that Jesus himself promised. But some people are just not willing to do what it takes to get there. Sticking around for an extra dessert is one thing, but persevering through hardships is quite another. But with your Holy Spirit to lead and guide, please help me be one who runs in such a way as to win the prize.

Miracles of Aging

"In Genesis, Eve messed up and ate the apple, then had the gall to encourage Adam to take a bite," said Karen S. God was so disappointed, Karen contends, that He promised some pretty severe consequences—such as pain in childbearing and having to answer to our husbands. And for the male population—well a life of work would be their fate.

Karen now believes, however, that God had a few other consequences on the back burner for the female of the species! Such as raising toddlers and teenagers, and then sticking us with menopause.

"Ah, good old menopause," Karen mused. "I no longer have to worry about getting pregnant. My husband and I can frolic anytime. No cramps or bloating. No tampons or shields or pads. The joy of it all." But as soon as the coast is clear and the kids are out—for good—well, Karen says the joke is on her. "My sex drive has diminished," she whispered. "And our 32-year-old son moved back home.

"Sometimes I think my husband would prefer the once-a-month ogre who menstruated and then got over it, to the unpredictable creature I've become since I hit menopause. He never knows what mood I'll be in. I'd let him know ahead of time—if I could. But I'm in the dark about my shifting moods as much as he is."

One minute, Karen admits, she is perspiring and fanning herself, and the next she reaches for a sweater to ward off the chill.

But menopause, according to Karen, is just one of many embarrassing aspects of aging. Millions of women would attest to the following. They come upon us when we least expect them.

As the growth of hair on our legs slows down, we realize we have plenty of time to care for our newly acquired mustaches. When we go in for a mammogram, we realize it's the only time anyone will ever ask us to appear topless—on film. Life has a way of throwing curves, and we are probably sitting on the biggest one of all.

As we age, we also begin to ponder the "big" questions in life, such as: "How much Healthy Choice ice cream can I eat before it's no longer a healthy choice?"

But there's comfort in this aging stuff, too—miracles actually, says Karen. Maybe our bodies have to expand a bit to hold all the love and wisdom and knowledge we've acquired.

Reflection

The fountain of wisdom is a bubbling brook (Proverbs 18:4).

Talking to God

Lord, as I walk through the grocery store, I see a whole section of foods whose packaging boasts healthy living. But even the most nutritious cereal or soup can only do so much for me. It can't keep me young. It can't control my mood swings. It can't keep away worry or fear. Only you can do those things for me through your love and patience and guidance. You are my fountain of youth and the author of my eternal life.

On the Warpath

Sue was excited. She had been invited to join a meeting planner for coffee at an upscale cafe in the city. They had not known each other before, but the man was someone Sue admired and hoped to do business with.

"Play it cool, but smart," Sue told herself. *This could lead to some new speaking engagements,* she thought as she dashed into the ladies room to touch up her hair and makeup.

Sue freshened her lipstick, then put a big red streak on each cheek, intending to blend them in before she left the restroom. A moment or two later, Sue walked out, purse over her shoulder, blouse tucked into her skirt, feeling confident. She patted her hair one last time as she walked over to the table where the meeting planner was waiting.

"We had a lovely late afternoon coffee and dessert," Sue reported. "We got acquainted, and then said good-bye. I drove home, feeling good about what we had accomplished. I walked into the bathroom, ready to strip my makeup and get into some comfortable clothes.

"I glanced in the mirror, and gasped in horror! Indian-on-warpath face! I had forgotten to blend the red stripes on my cheeks. The planner never said a word then or since, and I haven't, either."

Reflection

The unfading beauty of a gentle and quiet spirit, which is of great worth in God's sight (1 Peter 3:4).

Talking to God

Lord, how often do I sit across from you, assuming I look perfectly poised and put-together, only to discover later that my sins were as apparent as the blush on my cheeks. You didn't embarrass or condemn me. You allowed me to find out my true condition by looking at myself in a mirror. It is not a pretty picture. In fact, some days I appear so soiled there's no hope for me until I take a head-to-toe shower. Thank you for loving me even though I'm less than perfect.

Snow Bites and the Seven Dwarfettes

Once upon a time there lived a woman whose friends dubbed her Snow Bites (aka Shelley, the author of this tale). She had grown up in the frozen north, and whenever she stepped outdoors she often exclaimed, "Snow Bites!" Thus her nickname.

Snow decided one day that she'd had enough of the cold white stuff, so she moved south—to a warmer climate, and as the storyteller says, "she steeped herself in the ways of genteel Southern Belles. Or so she tried."

"Mirror, mirror on the wall," she often implored. "Who's the most delightful, clever, and engaging belle of all?'"

"Y'all are, ma'am," the mirror responded.

She continued living in this harmonious state until that fateful day when her hormones shifted, and she entered into a time of life known as menopause. "Snow Bites became one mad sister," said Shelley. "Then to make matters worse, out of nowhere appeared the Seven Dwarfettes: Crabby, Grouchy, Cranky, Ornery, Nasty, Mouthy, and Meany."

Suddenly everyone—living and dead—irritated Snow Bites. She told them off in no uncertain words. And "if no one was around," added Shelley, "Snow Bites would tell herself off!"

"Finally one day," said Shelley, "Snow entered the Land of Reality as she was having lunch with friends in a local restaurant. A little boy in the booth behind her stood up, turned suddenly, and poked her in the back with his fork. She felt like retaliating but he was just a little boy. *After all,* she told herself, *he was probably bored with his food and the adult conversation around him.* Snow caught herself before she did something she'd be ashamed of. It was "a small, but meaningful victory."

In that moment, Snow Bites began seeing for the first time in a long time what is important and true and worthwhile in life. She decided to take charge of the Seven Dwarfettes: Crabby, Grouchy, Cranky, Ornery, Nasty, Mouthy, and Meany. She kicked them out of her life that very day and told them never to come back. And that was final!

From that moment on, Snow/Shelley chose to live with peace and joy despite the circumstances. She knew without a doubt that God would see her through menopause—and beyond—for all eternity.

Reflection

Finally, brothers, whatever is true, whatever is noble, whatever is right, whatever is pure, whatever is lovely, whatever is admirable—if anything is excellent or praiseworthy—think about such things (Philippians 4:8).

Talking to God

What a blessing it is, O God, to know that even when Grumpy, Meany, Cranky, and Grouchy slip through the door of my life, you still love me. Your presence brings them out of hiding, and they quickly disappear. Then I can focus on what is right and true and pure and lovely.

Happy Birthday to Me!

"On my fortieth birthday our family took a vacation to Sea World," Donna shared. I was determined to prove that I was still as young and chipper as ever, so I stood in line with my husband and two of my sons to ride an enormous roller coaster called the Steel Eel.

"Once I boarded the car and started my slow ascent to the peak of the first hill, I realized that my fear of heights was a little stronger than I remembered. I squeezed my eyes shut and hung on for dear life."

Unknown to Donna at the time, the ride held a hidden camera that snaps a picture of the passengers at some point before they return. It's intended to capture the joy and exhilaration or the fear and terror, as the case may be, on the faces of each rider. As Donna and her family left the car at the end of the ride, a TV screen displayed their photo.

The family erupted in laughter at the sight of Donna's face contorted by fear and excitement. Donna's husband couldn't resist. He *had* to purchase the picture. He now shows it to friends, describing the photo of his wife as "the face of someone who's looked over the edge into the abyss and lived to tell about it. This," he says, "is what it looks like to be 40!"

If that wasn't enough, the family decided the following year to celebrate Donna's forty-first birthday with another unusual celebration. Her husband and five children and some close friends took her out for lunch after church one Sunday to a local restaurant.

Unknown to Donna at the time, "the tradition at this particular restaurant," she said, "was to stand the birthday girl on a chair in the middle of the restaurant so all of the patrons could sing 'Happy Birthday.'

"That particular Sunday, I had worn a shorter-than-usual skirt to church. The hemline just brushed the tops of my knees so it took several attempts for me to get up on the chair while maintaining my modesty. My husband, ever thoughtful, was in the back of the restaurant feeling embarrassed for me—but he didn't rush up to help me, either!"

Once Donna made it to the "throne," the young waiter, who was probably looking for a big tip, yelled, "May I have your attention please? I'd like everyone to sing 'Happy Birthday' to Donna, who is turning 21 today!"

"In a corner booth," said Donna, "some young whippersnapper took one look at me and proclaimed in a loud voice, 'No way!' That one remark burst any illusion I had about looking younger than I am!"

Reflection

May your father and mother be glad; may she who gave you birth rejoice (Proverbs 23:25).

Talking to God

Lord, I love it when people sing "Happy Birthday" to me. It's wonderful that friends and family want to celebrate the fact that I was born. But I want to celebrate you, O God, for you are the one who created me, who knit me together in my mother's womb. If you had not chosen me before the beginning of time, I would not be here today. Thank you for giving me life on earth and for the promise of eternal life in heaven.

Blondes Have
More Fun

One Sunday morning Lettie shampooed her hair. After towel drying it, she applied mousse. She had been using gel to bring it under control, but this particular day she decided to use a different product to see what results she'd get.

"As I was blow drying my hair, I couldn't help but notice how much body it had. *Why did I stop using this?* I wondered, already pleased with what I saw." Her hair dried beautifully, and it was so easy to manage. "I felt good about my hair all day," said Lettie.

She attended church and then went out to dinner with friends. When she returned home she was still delighted with how nice her hair had stayed all day and evening. She also noticed that it had more highlights than usual. It actually appeared lighter than her usual gray color.

By Monday morning, Lettie said it was definitely a golden color. Then she realized that something was terribly wrong. "What happened to my gray hair?" she muttered to herself. At that point she reached under the sink and pulled out the can she had used.

"Oh no!" she shouted. "Self-Tanning Skin Mousse!"

Lettie looked at herself in the mirror and laughed out loud. Then she checked the expiration date on the can: 1994! Way out of date. But it still worked! Lettie washed her hair several times that week, but there was no going back to gray. She was a blonde! Now to see if blondes really do have more fun!

A few days later Lettie attended the women's Christmas luncheon and party at her church. She gave the devotional program, as usual. She could tell heads were nodding as the women noticed her new "do." So she addressed the topic from the front of the room.

"Ladies," said Lettie, "I know you're too polite to ask, so I'll tell you what I did to my hair…." After relating her experience the audience broke into laughter. Then they shared their comments spontaneously.

"It's pretty. Looks really good."

"Very becoming."

"You should keep using the mousse."

"Yes. Pull it out of the trash."

"It matches your gold knit sweater."

A few days later, Lettie went to her hair dresser's. She was ready for her quarterly perm. The beautician was afraid to perm Lettie's hair because of the mousse. She wasn't sure the chemicals would mix appropriately.

Two weeks later Lettie returned.

"I'm not leaving here without a perm," she said. "If my hair turns green or orange or purple, just spray me with glitter and I'll sparkle!"

Fortunately, the perm did not damage Lettie's hair. In fact, she still has some of the blonde highlights. And she admits it's been a lot of fun!

Reflection

The king is enthralled by your beauty; honor him, for he is your lord (Psalm 45:11).

Talking to God

Lord, thank you that you love me regardless of the color of my hair, whether it's naturally curly, straight, or permed. You look at me from the inside out, and if I am living according to your will, then I am beautiful in your sight. Thank you for loving me just as I am.

Technophobia

Underdeveloped

At age 80, Miriam decided she had had quite enough challenges with picture-taking. She was fed up with complicated cameras that required focusing and adjusting and various lenses and special film and certain lighting to get just the right shot. What she needed in her old age was a simple point-and-shoot type that anyone could use. So you can imagine that she was first in line to purchase a disposable camera when they came onto the market.

With camera in hand, Miriam traveled to the Northwest to visit her son and family. She took lots of photos of various family members and all the outings they enjoyed at the beach, in the beautiful Redwoods, and in the mountains that surrounded the area.

Miriam finished the roll of film, then tossed the camera into a trash receptacle and headed down the road. A few days later she returned home eager to develop the film and share the results with her son and family. Then it hit her! She had been so focused on the ease of using a *disposable* camera that she went a step too far—disposing of the camera before developing the pictures!

Reflection

I will instruct you and teach you in the way you should go (Psalm 32:8).

Talking to God

Lord, when I look back on my life, I've done some pretty silly things, too. Maybe I'll spend more time listening for your instructions and less time relying on my own understanding. Then I'll know which way to go and what to do—even in the everyday details of my life.

Smoke Screen

"Now that Max and I no longer have to show our ID cards in order to qualify for the senior menu at IHOP or a senior discount at the movies," said Diana, "we've developed a sense of humor about the benefits and perils of growing older."

One year, a few weeks before Christmas, four of their grandchildren were spending the day with Diana and Max. The kids were helping their grandmother wrap gifts. One of the presents was a smoke alarm for their father, Diana's son.

"I asked if they had a smoke alarm in their house," said Diana. "They thought there was one, but no one seemed to know if it was still in good working order. I mentioned that ours wasn't working either."

Max overheard this brief conversation and decided to check theirs. "I'll have a look and test it," he said as he headed down the hall toward the spot where they had initially installed the alarm.

"The kids and I heard Max striking several matches," said Diana, "but nothing followed. A loud screech would have signaled that the alarm was working."

"Probably needs a new battery," Max hollered.

"What size does it take?" Diana called from the living room.

"That's funny," Max replied. "There's no place for a battery in this thing."

Diana could sense the frustration in his voice.

She and the kids walked down the hallway to see what was going on. Suddenly Max chuckled. Then they all burst into laughter as they realized Max had been holding the lighted matches under the ringer box for their electric doorbell.

"The smoke alarm was about five feet farther down the hall," said Diana. "He tested it, and it worked just fine."

Reflection

Teach me knowledge and good judgment, for I believe in your commands (Psalm 119:66).

Talking to God

I can't help but laugh, O Lord, when I make silly mistakes, especially when on second glance the right thing to do was so obvious. But sometimes my actions also scare me, especially as I'm growing older. I wonder if I'm beginning to lose it—or if I already have! Your Word saves me from these worries. You continually promise that you will give me the knowledge I need to make wise judgments. Thank you for that assurance.

Batteries Not Included

Roger stepped into the church his congregation had rented, and several volunteers greeted him. Then came the first of many challenges one hour before the Christmas program was to begin.

"There's no power," one woman sang out, followed by a chorus of new griefs.

"There's no heat in the sanctuary."

"The microphones don't work."

"Our turkey dinner will be cold."

As the director of Senior Ministries for the Union Gospel Mission of Seattle, Roger was in charge of *everything*. He hoped the problem would resolve itself. But just in case he actually could *do* something about it, he began his investigation of the power outage in the kitchen.

While there, Roger reached for a snack. The food looked and smelled so good. Hard to resist.

"Don't eat that," snapped Cindy, the food and kitchen coordinator, as she carefully guarded her freshly baked pumpkin pies. "The lights and outlets in the kitchen aren't working," she said with a raised eyebrow.

"Cindy kept watch over her pies," said Roger, "while she encouraged me to contact the custodian, Dorothy, who, by the way, was home with a newborn."

179

Dorothy lived two or three houses down from the church in a white house.

"I imagined myself as the fourth wiseman," added Roger, "as I went searching for the lady with the new baby. After considerable knocking, Dorothy came to the door. I spoke through the slight opening, introducing myself, and explaining that we had no power at the church."

"It's not my fault," said Dorothy, defending herself through the crack. "All I was told to do was unlock the front doors."

"Could you tell me where the electrical panel is located?" Roger asked.

"I can't be unlocking no rooms," she said.

"Hmmm, no rooms," Roger muttered under his breath, imagining what Joseph must have felt when the innkeeper told him there were no rooms available the night Jesus was born.

Roger dashed back to the church and called the senior pastor at his home to explain what had occurred. In a sleepy voice, the pastor said simply, "Well, the electricity was working fine yesterday."

Roger held his tongue and his rising temper! "Can you tell me where the electrical panel is located?" he asked.

"I have no idea," said the pastor.

Roger repeated the same conversation with the associate pastor and came up with the same result—nothing useful. Again, Roger's mind flashed back to the night of Christ's birth. *What if the original shepherds had not been watching their sheep?* he wondered. *What if they had ignored the angel's message and slept in?*

"That would have been baaad!" he said, enjoying the pun. "Well at least the angel had lights. We all know the 'glory of the Lord shown 'round them!'"

At that moment, Gary, Roger's supervisor, walked in.

"Is there anything I can do to help out?" he asked.

"Pray!" said Roger. He explained the situation to Gary, and the two men prayed. They implored heaven for electrical *and* spiritual power!

God responded quickly. One of the volunteers who had a knack with things electrical mentioned that one of the outlets in the hall was still working. So they ran an extension cord with power strips into the kitchen.

"And the Lord said, 'Let there be...hot apple cider,'" quipped Roger.

And it was good.

"The lights never did come on," said Roger, "except in my heart and mind. What I mean is that I realized that when we stay focused on Christ, He gives us the power we need, regardless of the circumstances."

Reflection

The LORD turns my darkness into light (2 Samuel 22:29).

Talking to God

I've been in some pretty dark places in my life, dear God. You above all, know how frightening that can be. I remember as a child, being afraid at night when the lights went out. And I remember as an adult, being afraid when the lights in my soul dimmed. I lost hope and courage and faith. But you rescued me from that pit by your grace and the promise in your Word that you would turn my darkness into light and my night into day. How you love me, O Lord. And how I love you!

Palm Reader

Judy and I became friends over the phone. I called her regarding some information I needed for one of my writing projects, and we were practically "buds" by the time we hung up. I remember wishing we lived closer so we could get together for a walk or tea or dinner with our husbands.

Once, after we hung up, I shot Judy an e-mail, thanking her for her time. She wrote back inviting my husband and me to visit if we ever came to Seattle. "Keep our phone number and address in your Palm Pilot," she said.

Oh no! I thought. *She assumes I have state-of-the-art technology—and I don't.* I was embarrassed to admit that I not only don't own a Palm Pilot, I'm not even sure what you do with one. I like the tried-and-true paper calendar.

I stewed for a moment or two and then decided to make light of it. "I don't have a Palm Pilot," I replied by e-mail. "But I have two palms. Does it count if I scribble your name and address on one of them? And make a copy on the other?"

Reflection

I thank my God every time I remember you (Philippians 1:3).

Talking to God

I am blessed with good friends, dear God. Thank you for them—those of many years and those new in my life. I want to keep in touch with them all, but that's impossible. You can help me, Lord, to remember them in prayer, at least. And if I can't recall every name, I can rest in the certainty that you know their names. By your Spirit not one will slip out from under your careful watch.

Cell-Phone Hunt

Cindy P. and her husband were remodeling their home. Thankfully, their daughter offered to help paint. She began the project, while Cindy ran to town to return some wallpaper samples and to run some errands.

"I told her we'd be back in about an hour," said Cindy. "I took my precious grandbaby Riley with me. Then I realized there was no way I could accomplish everything on my list in such a short time. Little ones need bathroom breaks, a treat at McDonald's, and maybe even a new toy!

"I decided to call my daughter to let her know I'd be away longer than I had promised. I reached for my cell phone, but it wasn't in its usual compartment in my purse. I had to use the phone in the wallpaper store."

When Cindy returned home, she looked for the phone where she thought she had seen it last, but it wasn't there. "Since stuff was so scattered throughout the house due to the home improvements, I was getting concerned that I had lost my cell phone."

"Mom," my daughter said, wanting to be helpful, "just call your cell number, and you'll be able to find it when it rings."

"Hey, great idea!" Cindy called the number and could hear it ringing. "It was so close," she added. "I began lifting boxes and looking behind stacks of clutter. I walked across the room, but still couldn't find it. From the sound I knew it was within reach. But where? It was maddening."

Then Cindy walked over to where her daughter was painting. "This is so odd," Cindy said. "No matter where I walk, even to the other end of the house, the sound is so close. *Where* is it? I'm getting frustrated."

"Mom," said her daughter in a knowing voice, "check your jacket pocket."

"There it was," said Cindy. "It had been with me the whole time!"

Reflection

Though seeing, they do not see (Matthew 13:13).

Talking to God

Lord, when I think of lost keys, a cell phone, sunglasses, or a myriad of other items, I'm amazed that I get through my day. It seems I'm always searching for one thing or another, especially as I get older. I put something down in one room, then move to another and lose track of where I put whatever it is I had in my hand. I look, but I don't see. Is that what I do with your Word, as well? Read the verses in Scripture but don't connect with their meaning? Or do I gloss over them without taking a moment to plant them in my heart so they are there when I need them? Help me today, dear Lord, to find new meaning in the word "seeing."

The Good
Old Days

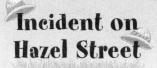

Incident on Hazel Street

"As the snow continues to develop on my roof and the fire dims in my basement," Lou joked, "I am noticing more signs of the aging process."

Lou's cousin Wanda had been visiting the church where Lou is the pastor. He had been out of touch with her and her family through the years, so he admitted he didn't know much about her. The visitor's card she signed revealed that she lived at 501 Hazel Street. "I knew she was divorced and had resumed using her maiden name, which is the same as mine—Jones," he added.

As Lou drove down Hazel Street, he spotted a house that he was certain was Wanda's. "I parked the car, walked to the door, and rang the bell," said Lou. "A rather husky gentleman in an unbuttoned khaki-colored shirt greeted me. I didn't know if he was a boyfriend, a neighbor, or a new husband!"

Lou introduced himself and said he was from the Saints Rest Missionary Baptist Church. "I'm stopping by today to say hello to Wanda. She's been visiting our church lately."

"Hello there," the man replied. "I'm Buck Bender. Come on in! Wanda isn't here today. She's gone to Denton to see the kids!"

Lou kept the tone light and friendly. "Well, Wanda and I are distant cousins," he said, smiling.

"Really? What side of the family?" asked Buck.

"The Jones side."

"Jones?" Buck looked puzzled. "My wife wasn't a Jones. She was a McDonald! But you've got the first name right. It's Wanda."

Suddenly Lou was a bit suspicious. "Is this address 501 Hazel Street?" he asked, feeling a bit embarrassed.

"No," said Buck. "It's 507. The little curly-q broke off the top of the number seven, so now it looks like a one."

Lou backed out the doorway and extended his hand. "Well, it's been real good visiting with you, Buck! And give my regards to Wanda—even if she's someone else's cousin!"

Reflection

Both the one who makes men holy and those who are made holy are of the same family (Hebrews 2:11).

Talking to God

Lord, it's a great feeling to know that when I walk in your kingdom I'm going to run into kin-folk wherever I go. They may not be blood relations, but they are my brothers and sisters in Christ. Thank you, God, for the gift of family here and ever after.

Golden Years My Foot!

appy New Year!" said Joyce to one of her geriatric patients.

"Are you kidding?" he replied in a gruff voice.

Joyce had clearly not intended to start her new year in such a frame of mind. She knew the man well. He had been a patient several times at the facility where she worked. During the summer he had fractured his hip, and in the spring he had been treated for a heart attack.

Joyce said the staff referred to him affectionately as the "frequent flyer." This particular time he was at the rehab center due to a severe case of pneumonia. He was too weak to return home from the hospital.

Joyce tried to cheer him up. "I'm sure this is not the 'get-away spot' of choice for your 'Golden Years,'" she sympathized.

"'Golden years'? What's so golden about them?" he shot back. "They should be called the rustin' years!"

Reflection

The fear of the LORD adds length to life (Proverbs 10:27).

Talking to God

Getting old sure ain't for wimps, Lord! I feel scared sometimes—especially when I'm sick—but then I think of your promises. You've said you will be with me always and that you will give me a long and full life when I walk in your ways and trust in you alone. I believe you!

Christmas Surprise

How would you like to come here for Christmas?"
Millie B.'s daughter Shirley, who lives in Canada, issued
the invitation one November years ago. She even offered to
buy her parents' airplane tickets.

"Thanks, but no, thanks," Millie replied.

She and her husband had retired and moved from Iowa
to Arizona to escape the cold and snow. "There was no way
we would consider going to Canada in December. Even
Canadian geese fly south for the winter!" Millie shared later.

They resigned themselves to another Christmas without
their daughter and son-in-law, Mike. They had already been
separated for nine years when the younger couple served as
missionaries in South America, so it wasn't anything new.

The day before Christmas the doorbell rang and Millie
answered it. "No one was there—just a huge refrigerator
carton. No car or delivery van was in sight. I called for my
husband to come."

The couple walked outside and circled the box. "It was
addressed to us but had no return label," Millie continued.
"Puzzled, I pushed on it and then jumped back, startled.
'Something moved in there!' " I exclaimed.

"Suddenly the top of the box flew open, and two familiar
heads popped up. 'Merry Christmas!' " shouted Shirley and
Mike as they held out their arms to us.

"What a surprise it was—fun and funny at the same time! It was too good to keep to ourselves," said Millie. "After we had visited awhile, we decided to drive to our son's home to surprise his family also. We tied the carton onto the top of our car and slowly drove the 15 miles to Scottsdale. By the time we arrived there, it was nearly dark. We parked half a block away from the house. Shirley and Mike positioned themselves inside the box on the front walk and my husband and I selected our hiding place in the shrubbery. This time I had the fun of sneaking up to ring the doorbell, then dashing back out of sight."

Their daughter-in-law, Carol, came to the door and when she saw the box, she called the rest of the family. As they stared at the huge carton, it moved slightly and Carol remarked, "I don't think I want to open this. We don't need another pet."

"By that time," said Millie, "we couldn't keep our secret another minute. We began laughing as Shirley and Mike again popped out with their joyous, 'Merry Christmas!'"

They all enjoyed a never-to-be-forgotten family Christmas!

Reflection

They ate and drank with great joy in the presence of the LORD that day (1 Chronicles 29:22).

Talking to God

Lord, what a great blessing it is to share holidays with my family—especially Christmas, when we have the privilege of celebrating the

*birth of Jesus. Thank you for the gift of parents
and children and grandchildren. Thank you also
for the joy we feel when we are together, eating
and drinking and playing in your holy presence.*

Fifty Cents for Seniors

Pam and David's car went kaput. Service was needed, so they made arrangements to take their vehicle to the Dodge dealership for repairs. That meant Pam would be riding the bus for the first time in many years—an experience in itself.

Pam found out the schedule and where to wait. She bundled up against the cold Oregon weather and headed out for no more of a walk than her daily exercise routine. *So far so good,* she thought. With coins in hand, she stood at the bus stop. Then suddenly she spied the bus lights in the morning fog. She was eager to board, find a seat, and be on her way.

Then it occurred to her: "How much is the fare? When do I pay? At boarding time or as I depart?" She felt a bit nervous since this was her first ride in a long time.

The big doors opened and Pam stepped up and through the rear door of the bus. She thought she heard the driver mumble something in her direction, but she didn't catch it so she sat down, assuming she'd pay when she reached her destination.

Suddenly Pam realized the bus driver was glaring at her and motioning her forward. "You!" the woman shouted, as though Pam were the target in a criminal lineup. "Are you going to pay or do you think this is a free ride?"

Pam was mortified. She certainly didn't intend to cheat anyone—and certainly not the city transportation system. She explained to the driver her misconception about when to pay. The driver had no pity. "Well, you better get it straight, now," she bellowed. "Some other driver could give you a terrible time!"

What is this, if not a hard time? Pam wondered.

Pam asked the fee. "You a senior?" the driver asked.

Pam nodded yes.

"Fifty cents for seniors," the driver said flatly.

Pam plunked her coins into the machine and walked down the aisle toward her seat, certain an undercover agent would surely leap out, trip her, and cuff her! But nothing unexpected occurred. Pam settled in for the ride, feeling a mix of anger, embarrassment, and fear. But she didn't give in to any of those little demons!

She decided to give kindness for curtness. When she arrived at her destination, Pam held her head high, walked to the front of the bus, looked the driver in the eye, and said in a kind voice: "Thanks for your help. Have a good day."

The driver mumbled something unintelligible and roared away from the curb.

Pam walked away with a smile on her face. She had to admit the price was right. Fifty cents for a bus ride with a bonus—a reminder to practice the Golden Rule regardless of the circumstances.

Reflection

Do to others as you would have them do to you (Luke 6:31).

Talking to God

When people are rude to me, Lord, I feel like retaliating. Why should I extend myself when they don't care about me? Then I'm reminded of your love for me. I don't always show respect and love for you. My thoughts and words and actions are often mean-spirited and defensive. And yet you continue to love and forgive me. Help me to be more like you, dear God, and to treat others as you treat me—regardless of the situation.

Moving
Forward

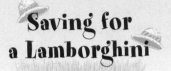

Saving for a Lamborghini

While growing up, Susan and her siblings heard not once, not twice, but dozens of time, a stern reminder from their father to communicate clearly. "We were told again every time there was a mixup over the use of the family car or over whose turn it was to wash the dishes and whose turn it was to dry," said Susan. "If I had a nickel for every time I heard Dad's sage words, I'd be driving a Lamborghini."

From kids to seniors, poor communication is rampant in today's fast-paced Internet society. "We leave out words that convey detail," Susan added. "We don't complete sentences—and some of us even go so far as to utter one-word replies, assuming others understand our meaning."

Here's an example of a conversation Susan overheard in an employee lunchroom.

"You finish that project yet?"

"Nope, boss hasn't kinda given me all the numbers."

"Well, ya know, I mean, what does he expect you to do?"

"Hang."

"Hang?" Susan asks. "I envision the poor employee dangling from the ceiling by his necktie because he can't meet his deadline due to missing information from his boss. What he means, of course, is that he'll just have to wait.

"Ka-ching. Another nickel in my Lamborghini fund."

Despite her father's warning to say clearly what one means and to mean what one says, misunderstandings still prevail in Susan's family. "My husband is the worst offender," acknowledged Susan, "but then English is his *third* language so..."

Shortly before Easter some years ago, Susan understood her husband to say they were out of eggs, but he didn't have time to stop by the farmers market to buy more.

So Susan went to the market. And so did her husband. "I guess I misunderstood him," she said. "The conversation about how four dozen eggs accumulated in our refrigerator led to talking about taking a trip to Europe over Easter break to visit my husband's relatives."

Susan started packing only to learn just before zipping up the last bag that her husband was merely *thinking* about it. He hadn't actually decided. "In addition to all the washing, ironing, and planning for the trip," said Susan, "I had given away the four dozen eggs. So there we were— staying home and once again out of eggs! The Lamborghini fund gained five nickels for that bit of miscommunication."

Recently Susan added another five cents when her friends Andrea and Larry returned home for their annual summer leave from their overseas government jobs. Susan and her husband get together with the couple at least one time during every leave. And they planned to do the same that year.

"Dinner at an American pub is always a treat for Larry and Andrea," said Susan. To add to the festive night, Susan contacted her brother Herb, who is always on the prowl for a new and better pub. She asked for a recommendation. As expected, he and his wife Mary had discovered yet another mini-brewery.

Susan was excited about introducing their friends to this new spot that was famous for brew and great food. "Can you make it Friday evening at six-thirty?" Susan asked Andrea. "Invite your parents to come along, too," she added. "We'd love to see them again."

"Sounds great, but we need directions," replied Andrea.

"I'll have my brother call you on this," said Susan, "since I have no idea how to get there."

"Okay then, we'll see you in Kutztown on Friday at six-thirty," Andrea confirmed.

Herb went so far as to drive to Andrea's house to drop off the written directions. What a nice guy! As he pulled away from the curb, he shouted his parting words. "I've made reservations for eight. See you Friday in Kutztown."

"We did see our friends and their parents," said Susan. "*Eventually!* They showed up at the restaurant on Friday evening shortly before eight, a bit testy and very hungry."

"We're so glad you're here already," Andrea's mother Joyce told Susan as she sat down. "We senior citizens aren't used to eating this late. The guys are practically starving. Why did you change the time?" she queried.

"I didn't change the time," said Susan. "We arrived at six-thirty as we agreed." Susan could feel her face grow warm with irritation. *Our friends show up over an hour late,* she thought to herself, *and then ask why we changed the time? Hel-lo!*

"*Who* changed the time?" Susan asked, staring down at Herb like an enraged general. At that point she was sure she heard the faint sound of a nickel dropping into her Lamborghini fund!

"Herb. Herb changed the time," the four latecomers shouted at once, pointing accusative fingers at him.

"I most certainly did not," Herb said defending himself. "Joyce, I told you I made reservations for eight, just to be sure you understood that you and Eddie were included."

"All eight of us had a good laugh at Herb's expense," said Susan, "when we realized how something as simple as the time of day and the number of guests could be misunderstood because of the shortcuts we take in our daily communications. If this trend continues, I'll soon be driving that new car."

Reflection

Trust in the LORD with all your heart and lean not on your own understanding (Proverbs 3:5).

Talking to God

I really like this proverb, dear God. We both know how much trouble I've gotten myself into when I lean on my own understanding! I'd rather forget about it, actually. I'm learning, though. My entire life works so much better when I trust in you with all my heart. Help me, dear God, to do just that.

Milestone Birthday

Janice just celebrated the big 5-0! About a week before the blessed event, her eldest son asked, "So, how old will you be, Mom?"

"Fifty," Janice responded, trying to sound positive.

Her younger son cringed. "Yuck. Sounds old."

"Leave it to a teenager," said Janice. "He reduced a life crisis down to three words!

"I went out of town for a few days following my birthday and enjoyed a week of feeling special. Then I returned home to find that my sons had dirtied every plate, cup, fork, knife, and spoon in the house. They even used the Christmas glasses!

"They also wore every piece of clothing they owned and dumped all their laundry in the kitchen. So much for feeling special!" It was back to business as usual.

On her actual birthday, Janice's husband, Jim, took her to a fancy restaurant. "He's an artist manager in Nashville," she said, "and one of his artists had given him a gift certificate to a steak house as a Christmas gift. So in July, he decided to use it for my birthday. Not that he's cheap or anything!"

After a lovely dinner and dessert, Janice excused herself and walked to the ladies room. "I was feeling pretty good about myself," she said, as she glanced in the mirror. "Not bad for 50!"

"Afterwards I sashayed down the hall in my slinky black dress right in to the main dining room where I heard dance music playing. I dipped and twirled on my way back to our table—but slipped and fell before I reached it! Two young waiters sailed across the floor to rescue me."

"Are you all right, ma'am?" one of them asked as the other reached to help me up.

"Nothing was hurt but my ego," Janice admitted. "I smiled weakly. I'm all right," I replied. "I'm just...well, 50. Sounds old, doesn't it?"

Reflection

From six calamities he will rescue you (Job 5:19).

Talking to God

Lord, I have to admit it's a kick to get older. I feel more freedom to do outrageous things, such as turn a cartwheel on the front lawn with my grandchildren, swing dance with my husband (like Mom and Dad used to do), or rock climb with my grandson. I've been much "too" appropriate in my life. It's time to make a splash and enjoy this precious life you've given me.

Time to Move

Edith decided in her early eighties that it was time to sell her family home and move to smaller quarters. Roger, from the Seniors Ministry at her church, offered to help organize her possessions and pack up what she planned to take with her. As the two moved toward a collection of books, Roger picked up a volume and leafed through it.

"There's a funny story behind that book," said Edith whimsically. "When my husband Hubert was still alive, he filled our basement with books," she added, rolling her eyes at just the thought of the overwhelming personal library he had amassed without her agreement.

"Years ago one of our neighbors was planning a fund-raiser garage sale. She was collecting old books from everyone on the block. I quickly packed up three boxes of our books and gave them to her, but I never told Hubert," Edith said, chuckling.

The morning of the sale, Edith and Hubert paid a visit to their neighbor's garage to support her effort to raise charitable funds. As they walked through the rows of books, Edith suddenly heard Hubert shout from across the room.

"Oh, Momma," he called, raising a particular book in his hand.

"Look!" proclaimed Hubert, "it's that book I've been wanting for so long!"

Edith couldn't help but laugh all over again. "Roger, it was the very book you're holding now," she said. "One from Hubert's own collection. He snatched up the copy and walked right over to the cashier and plunked down his money—paying for the book a second time. I never did tell him that he bought back his own book," said Edith. "And I'm not sure to this day, he ever read it."

Reflection

For in him we live and move and have our being (Acts 17:28).

Talking to God

Moving can be a good thing—though it's hard to give up the familiar. But I think it's important to stay in reality, especially as I get older. I don't need as much space as I used to. And I can get along with fewer possessions. I thank you for the large home we had when our family needed it. But now I can be content wherever I live as long as you are with me and I am with you.

Changes

Carol admits that growing old is not so bad—especially when you consider the alternative. She likes to remember the old saying, "Age is mostly a matter of mind. If you don't mind, it doesn't matter."

Some of the changes in the world around her, however, do bother her. "For example," she asks, "why have the clothing manufacturers changed their sizing scale? What used to be a size 12 dress is now a size 16. Didn't they think we would notice these things? I'm also convinced that people who make bathroom scales have also changed their dials. There's no way I'd ever let myself weigh as much as my scale registers!"

Carol has also observed that department store clerks have started whispering. "I don't know why this sudden change," she says bewildered. She could hear them just fine ten years ago!

Getting old ain't for wimps—it's true. In fact, getting older, period, is not really the problem. It's all the other stuff going on around us. "Have you gone up a flight of stairs recently?" asks Carol. "They're making them a lot steeper than they used to. I can remember when going up a flight of stairs was nothing. Now they're so steep I have to stop halfway to catch my breath."

Carol has a few comments, as well, about how fast people drive these days. She and her daughter were out one day together, and it was so dangerous even her daughter had white knuckles. "She cautioned me," said Carol, "to look in the rearview mirror before I pulled onto the highway.

"I reminded her of my impeccable driving record," said Carol. "But the next time I was out I did look in the mirror, and all I have to say is, it's a good thing cars have brakes. The way *other* people screeched and swerved around me, it's no wonder there are so many accidents these days."

Growing older does require some preparation. "It's the responsible thing to do," claims Carol. She and her husband put their financial affairs in order and drew up a family trust.

"I thought everything went well, until we were finishing up and our oldest daughter turned to her dad and said, 'Daddy, please don't die first and leave her for us to take care of.'

"The older I get, the one thing that bothers me the most," said Carol, "is that my friends in heaven will think I didn't make it."

Reflection

He changes times and seasons; he sets up kings and deposes them. He gives wisdom to the wise and knowledge to the discerning (Daniel 2:21).

Talking to God

Lord, thanks so much for being on my team even when my fellow "teammates" shake their heads and chuckle at my behavior. Sometimes I get exasperated with myself, too. I'd like to be able to sail up the stairs as I used to, see a lower number on the scale when I weigh myself, drive and talk at the same time without risking the safety of those with me, but I can't do what I once did. Times are a-changing and I must go with the flow of getting older. I pray for continued wisdom and discernment now and in the days and years ahead.

Creative
Cookery

Home Cooking with a Twist

Maureen invited her neighbors, Pat and Ted, over for dinner. They had helped with some gardening projects, and this was her way of saying more than thank you. She wanted to cook her famous recipe for southern spare ribs—the ones everyone talked about.

That afternoon, before her company arrived, she dusted the furniture, tidied the bathrooms, vacuumed the carpets, and set the table. She even used her best china and the silverware her mother had left her. Maureen wanted her friends to know how much they mattered to her. What would she do without such good people to help her out when she was in need?

At four o'clock sharp, Maureen took the baby back ribs out of the refrigerator, laid them in a glass baking dish, and seasoned them with salt and pepper and a squirt of lemon juice to give them just the right bite. Then she pulled out a bottle of barbecue sauce. She didn't have her glasses handy so she couldn't read the label; she relied on the shape of the container to tell what was in it. She had used this sauce so often before, she knew the bottle by feel.

Maureen poured the liquid over the ribs, then smoothed it just right with a spatula so every rib was generously covered.

She carefully placed the glass pan in the oven and set the timer. While the ribs cooked she prepared a salad and vegetable and heated the dinner rolls in the bread warmer.

At five-thirty the doorbell rang, and Maureen hurried to answer it. She greeted Pat and Ted and ushered them into the living room. "Thank you for having us," said Pat. "This is a real treat after a long day at work."

Ted agreed. "I've been looking forward to this meal ever since you invited us," he said. "I hear you're famous for baby back ribs. And I understand your sauce is the best."

After a round of fruit punch and a plate of crackers and cheese, Maureen invited them to the table. She set the platter of ribs, the bowl of vegetables, and the warm rolls on the serving cart. Then she tossed the salad with a light vinegarette dressing.

Ted went right for the ribs. "May I use my fingers?" he asked.

"Be my guest," said Maureen. "People have told me my ribs are finger-lickin' good! Let me know what you think," she added, laughing.

Ted took a bite, then looked up, his eyes wide. He seemed at a loss for words.

"Is anything wrong?" asked Maureen, her heart pounding.

"No, no. Everything's fine," said Ted. "Maybe it's this cold I'm trying to kick. It seems to have affected my taste buds. I could swear the ribs are covered in chocolate sauce."

Maureen rushed from the table to the trash container in the kitchen. This time she put on her glasses first. Sure enough. The empty container which she thought had held her famous barbecue sauce said in plain English: Hershey's Chocolate Sauce.

Maureen felt like a wimp! But she didn't let on. Instead she took a deep breath and made the best of an embarrassing moment. "If you think my ribs are great," she said, "wait till you see what I have for dessert—ice cream sundaes topped with barbecue sauce!"

Reflection

With humility comes wisdom (Proverbs 11:2).

Talking to God

Dear Lord, it's funny—but it's also kind of scary when we start doing things we've never done before! At times like this I'm grateful for a sense of humor. It might take a minute for me to laugh at myself, but I feel better when I do. It seems I need a good dose of humility each day as much as I need my daily vitamins!

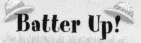

Batter Up!

My friend Olga works full-time in the family business. Her daughter Elizabeth is in high school. They both have consuming schedules, so it's a rare occasion when they simply hang out together in the kitchen being domestic. But one day before Christmas that's exactly what they did.

Elizabeth loved having her mom at her side as the two mixed batter for muffins and cookies. It was a sweet moment between them—so sweet that Elizabeth, in a moment of gratitude, reached out to hug her mother.

Olga was touched by the spontaneous gesture, but in that second she realized her hands were gooey with moist batter. She didn't want to soil Elizabeth's outfit, so she didn't hug her back.

Later, Olga shared this experience with me and a couple of women friends. One piped up, "So what if you got a little batter on her blouse? That was a precious moment between the two of you. You can always wash a blouse."

I could tell by the look on Olga's face that she wished she had just hugged Elizabeth and said to heck with the mess it might have caused.

I think she made the right decision, however. After all, if anyone had been looking in the kitchen window, he or she might have called Child Protective Services, reporting that a mother has just "battered" her child!

Reflection

Train a child in the way he should go, and when
he is old he will not turn from it (Proverbs
22:6).

Talking to God

*Lord, our children and grandchildren are such a
blessing. Thank you for our times together,
learning, growing, hugging, playing, praying,
cooking. My life is so much richer for having
these beautiful people to love and care about.
May I never lose sight of the gift of family.*

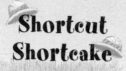

Shortcut Shortcake

In early summer, Barbara bought a tub of strawberry glaze at the supermarket anticipating making a fresh strawberry pie. She could almost taste the succulent berries topped with *real* whipped cream and drizzled with glaze.

"I have a perfectly delicious and easy-to-make recipe for glaze," she said, "but that day the 'prepared' glaze seemed like the better choice."

Barbara returned home and put the tub of glaze in a safe place in her pantry. She'd have it ready to use on baking day. One thing and another came up, however, and a few weeks passed.

Then one day she noticed a special sale at the market. A four-pound container of fresh strawberries for a great price. Barbara knew she'd have more berries than she needed for the pie, so she picked up a package of dessert cups for strawberry shortcake, along with the four pounds of berries.

"When I arrived home," said Barbara, "I put the dessert cups in a safe place, as well. Now I had everything I needed for strawberry pie and strawberry shortcake." She could hardly wait to taste these delicious summer desserts.

A couple of days later, she was ready to make the pie. "I searched every shelf of the pantry and even all my cupboards," said Barbara, "but I couldn't find the glaze anywhere."

Barbara knew the berries wouldn't keep so she served them for breakfast, in fruit salads, and for snacks. Soon there were no longer enough berries for a pie. "I remembered the dessert cups," she said, "and decided that would be a good alternative. We'd have strawberry shortcake for dessert that evening."

Wouldn't you know, she couldn't find the dessert cups either. Her ability to find a safe place was beyond her ability to remember what it was!

She would not be daunted. Barbara began another earnest search for the hidden glaze and dessert cups. Out of options, she even asked her husband if he'd seen either one. "He had no clue," said Barbara, "so I was on my own again."

They continued to eat the remaining berries and when they were just about gone, Barbara spotted the tub of glaze in the pantry. She had no idea why she hadn't noticed it before when she needed it.

"By then," said Barbara, "the strawberry season was about over. The berries were declining in quality and increasing in price. I decided to forget the pie."

Since then Barbara committed herself to using the glaze next year—that is, if she can find it. And what became of the dessert cups? They, too, showed up the day after the last berry had been eaten. They had fallen to the back of the bottom shelf.

"Oh well," said Barbara. "It won't be long till it's peach season—and peach shortcake is one of my favorites. Now where did I put that glaze again?"

Reflection

For the kingdom of God is not a matter of eating and drinking, but of righteousness, peace and joy in the Holy Spirit (Romans 14:17).

Talking to God

Lord, I can relate to this story. I buy something, put it away for safekeeping, and then when I need it, I can't find it. I'm obviously better at hiding than finding. If I keep this up, it's going to be Meals on Wheels for me! Please help me to be conscious of each action I take. Help me also to trust you, since I'm bound to make mistakes. Let me find joy in you first—and then in eating and drinking.

Cheese Popcorn

One night Cheryl felt an overwhelming desire to have some cheese popcorn, a weakness of hers, she admitted. "My husband, Griff, was asleep on the couch." *Perfect timing!* she thought. *I can have the whole bag to myself.*

Cheryl waited till late at night—on purpose—so she wouldn't have to listen to her husband remind her of the deal they'd made about eating more healthfully and losing weight. Cheryl wanted to give in to her urge so she asked God for help.

"I expected Him to remove the desire," she said, "but it remained, so I went with it. I popped the corn and watched Griff closely. He moved a little but the sound didn't wake him up. *Yippee!*"

But he did awaken as soon as the last kernel popped. Cheryl left the popcorn in the kitchen and sat near her husband on the sofa waiting for him to come to. He seemed to be in a sleepy trance so Cheryl decided she had time to enjoy her snack. She carried the bowl into the living room and sat down on the other end of the couch.

"Without saying a word Griff suddenly reached over and began eating my popcorn," said Cheryl. "Not just a few kernels either, but big, man-sized handfuls! One after another.

He was gorging on it! I wanted to say *Stop!* or *Get out of my bowl!* or just plain *Nooooo!* But the words wouldn't come."

Cheryl sat there taking deep breaths, trying to remain calm as Griff continued eating. "I could almost see the bottom of the bowl," she said, "and I couldn't pop more because that was the last bag in the pantry!"

After a few moments, Cheryl came to her senses. She realized that God did, in fact, save her from herself. "He certainly has a sense of humor," she added. "Maybe next time he won't have to go to such lengths to get my attention!"

Reflection

Food eaten in secret is delicious! (Proverbs 9:17).

Talking to God

I've eaten in secret more than once. Remember the time I ate half the chocolate cake when no one was looking? Or the time I hid a candy bar for later, and then it was missing when I reached for it? Apparently someone else in this family likes to eat when no one else is around. I need to look at my own habits with food. Why don't I want to share the treats? Why do I like to eat in secret? Hmmm. Am I lonely or scared or fearful or resistant about something and using food to dull the feelings? Lord, please show me what this means about me.

Dinner at Five

Vic Camp's parents lived with him and his wife Barbara Jean (B.J.) in California for 10 years in an apartment built especially for them on the lower level of the Camps' home. They paid rent as tenants, yet had the safety and convenience of being in the same house with their son and his family.

Noonie, Vic's mother, did not drive, but she loved to go out with B.J., who was working as an interior designer and often had a variety of stops to make. While out for the day, they'd stop at a nice restaurant and have lunch—something Noonie always looked forward to.

One day as they were out and about, Noonie suddenly realized it was nearly 5:00 P.M.—the time she and her husband ate dinner each night.

"I can't stay out any longer," she said to B.J. "In fact, I should have been home by four o'clock."

"Why?" asked B.J.

"Pa wants me home by then to get dinner ready by five."

"It was too early for me to end my work day," said B.J., but that day she made an exception and took Noonie home. When they arrived, B.J. approached her father-in-law. "Pa, does it really matter to you that Noonie be home by four when she's out with me?"

225

"Not at all," he said amiably. "Stay out as long as you need to—just so we eat by five!"

Reflection

Life is more than food, and the body more than clothes (Luke 12:23).

Talking to God

Aren't we a funny bunch, dear Lord? We want what we want when we want it. Period. I think I'm generous and loving, and I suppose I am— to a point—the point when what someone else needs and wants from me interferes with what I want and need. This is a big issue. I need to spend some time looking at that and evaluating my attitude. Thank you for teaching me that following your way is more important than getting my way.

City-Grown Eggs

"My parents form a perfect composite of the left and right brain," Millie commented. "Mom is the artistic music educator, and Dad is the engineer. When I was 10, living in metropolitan Manila, my mother hatched the idea of raising chickens. She wanted us to enjoy fresh eggs even though she knew nothing about raising chickens in our upper-middle class neighborhood."

Millie's dad didn't know anything about it, either, but together they forged ahead with no previous experience or information!

To start with, her engineer father designed a state-of-the-art chicken coop for the backyard, one large enough to hold about 50 cluck-clucks. "He designed it so the eggs would roll down a slanted floor to a collection trough."

Millie and her sister got into the act, as well. They named one of their favorite hens Fred, and together the girls collected eggs—about a dozen in all. Soon the project became a real chore for the entire family. "The chickens were dirty, and the rooster woke us up every morning," said Millie.

Then one day while Millie's dad was away on business, a typhoon brought a disease that attacked the family's chickens.

With advice from Millie's uncle, her mother received instructions on how to dispose of the diseased poultry. Millie and her sister listened in. They were horrified.

"That evening our dinner table was quiet and somber," said Millie. "Dad had returned. We stared at the bowls in front of us in grief and disgust. What used to be Fred's leg was floating in broth with some vegetables. Right then I wanted to protest Fred's murder by declaring that I was a vegetarian."

The girls' mother prompted them to eat. They stared at their father for guidance. He took one bite of Fred's leg and announced, "This is tough."

"It's tough," the girls repeated in case their mother didn't get the message.

Their mother sighed in disgust and then opened up cans of pork and beans for dinner.

Reflection

I have food to eat that you know nothing about (John 4:32).

Talking to God

Lord, I have a lot going on about food—where it comes from, how it's cooked, what it looks like, and how it tastes. Food. Food. Food. It's about time I stop focusing on what I put into my body and pay closer attention to taking in the food you offer—the bread of eternal life.

Breakfast in the Bathroom

You've heard of *Breakfast at Tiffany's*—the movie with Audrey Hepburn. Well my husband and I have our own version: *Breakfast in the Bathroom*. The drama started a month ago when we decided to upgrade our 25-year-old kitchen.

With dedication and excitement, we signed the contract with a kitchen designer. Then we unloaded every knife, fork, and spoon, plate, cup, and dish, appliance, box, and bag and a thousand other things from all the cabinets, drawers, and pantry. The living and dining rooms were now a warehouse of kitchen clutter.

"You'll be up and running again in about ten days to two weeks," said the foreman on the job.

It's been a month—and we're still eating breakfast in the bathroom! Our fold-up aluminum picnic table, straddling the edge of the bathtub, is a holding place for protein powder, bread, butter, hard-boiled eggs, vitamins and assorted snacks. We can't use the bathtub now—but at least the shower works. Paper plates and cups are stacked on the floor between the two sinks. And the toaster sits atop the portable microwave oven that sits atop the tile bench seat beside the bathtub!

Actually, it's pretty convenient. We can draw water from the tub faucet, heat it in the microwave for tea or coffee, pop a slice of bread into the toaster while cutting up hard-boiled eggs and whipping up a banana-berry protein drink. Then we pull up a seat on the floor, eat, drink, and hop into the shower, rinsing the dishes as we rinse ourselves! This may be an entirely new concept. I wonder if we could make money on it—enough to pay for the kitchen upgrade!

Reflection

Jesus said to them, "Come and have breakfast." None of the disciples dared ask him, "Who are you?" They knew it was the Lord (John 21:12).

Talking to God

Lord, what was it like to have breakfast with you? I would love to have been there, eating and drinking and talking with you as we broke our night fast and replenished our bodies for the new day. Even though I cannot pull up a chair at your table, I can still receive your daily bread each morning through prayer and meditation. When you fill my cup, I'm ready to take on the day as you have ordained.

Close-Ups

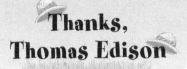

Thanks, Thomas Edison

Joan and her husband, John, have a special friend who is now 80 years of age. One weekend the couple invited her to join them for a visit to the Anza-Borrego Desert.

She was the perfect guest, ready to help out wherever needed—especially in the kitchen. As Joan prepared one of their meals, she turned around to say something to her friend who was busy fanning the stove.

"What are you doing?" Joan asked, puzzled.

"Trying to get this stove to start," the woman responded, a bit perplexed.

The two burst out laughing when Joan's elderly friend suddenly realized the stove was electric, not gas.

Reflection

I am with you to rescue and save you (Jeremiah 15:20).

Talking to God

Lord, you must chuckle at the sight of me some-times. I do such silly things. When I wake up to them I'm sure I turn red. But I never need to worry that you will leave me over them. You encourage me to laugh and make the most of life. You'll be there—no matter what—and you'll always help me recover from even the most humiliating moment.

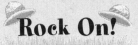Rock On!

Nearly every day Mary walks by a beautiful row of olive trees and boulders. It's become part of her exercise routine. One morning as she walked along, caught up in her own little world of thoughts and musings, she noticed a giant boulder.

Why it's as big as a VW Bug, she thought. The limb of an adjacent tree was crowded up against it—with nowhere to go or grow. Suddenly Mary muttered under her breath as she passed by, "Wow. If that rock gets any bigger, it's going to crush the tree...."

Reflection

He is the Rock, his works are perfect, and all his ways are just (Deuteronomy 32:4).

Talking to God

You're my Rock, Lord, unshakable, immovable, unfathomable. I never need worry that you will move or change because you will not. You'll take care of me and all your creation from now till the end of time. I am so grateful to be able to stand on you, the Rock of my salvation.

Birth of a Joke

Sherry says she loves to hear her mother tell a joke. "Mom cracks up while telling it, but then she sobers up at the end...because she can't remember the punchline!

"On one such occasion," said Sherry, "she was telling a joke to a man she had met while we were on vacation. Once again she laughed through the telling about some older women who were losing their memories. Sure enough she got to the end and realized the same thing was happening to her. She couldn't remember the punchline."

Those sitting around listening gave her a moment or two to remember. Finally, she had it—but it came so late the joke went flat. Everyone laughed, but more at Sherry's mother than at the joke.

"The gentleman asked Mom if she knew how to spell the word *gullible*. Mom thought it was the start of a joke," Sherry said, "so she giggled as she tried to come up with the proper spelling. After a few seconds, she spelled it correctly. The gentleman told her it was a good thing she knew because that word had been removed from the dictionary."

"Are you serious?" Sherry's mom asked.

"Yep," the man responded dead serious. Then everyone erupted in laughter. She had not only spelled the word correctly, she had modeled the definition perfectly!

Reflection

The unfolding of your words gives light; it gives understanding to the simple (Psalm 119:130).

Talking to God

Lord, thank you that when words fail me and understanding seems far away, you provide the words I need to light my way and you simplify what has been complicated. I am grateful that I can trust you to provide what I need when I need it.

Now and Then

My mother read somewhere that people live in the "now and then" instead of in the "here and now." But of herself, she said, "*I* live in the here and now, now and then!"

A bit of doggerel poetry penned in her journal during her last decade on earth, however, also points out that as her life drew to a close, she thought about "then" more and more.

One Pilgrim's Progress

From year to year we travelled
Thinking all the way...
Will God be there to greet us?
And will we want to stay?
To sit with Him and show our love,
Is what we have in mind.
He's been so good and loving
None better could we find!

Mrs. Eva O'Connor

Reflection

[God] has made everything beautiful in its time. He has also set eternity in the hearts of men; yet they cannot fathom what God has done from beginning to end (Ecclesiastes 3:11).

Talking to God

Dear Lord, at the end of the road on earth, let me focus my eyes on the path to heaven and trust that you will guide me and my glad and thankful heart into your kingdom.